A Macroeconomics Workbook

Also by G. F. Stanlake:

First Economics
First Economics Answer Book
Introductory Economics
Introductory Economics Workbook
Macroeconomics: an Introduction
Objective Tests in Economics
Public Finance (*Longman Economic Studies* series)

Also by B. Harrison:
Pricing and Competition in the Private Sector (*Longman Economic Studies* series)

A Macroeconomics Workbook

GF Stanlake MA BSc(Econ)

B Harrison BA

LONGMAN GROUP LIMITED
Longman House, Burnt Mill, Harlow, Essex CM20 2JE, England
and Associated Companies throughout the World

First published 1984
ISBN 0 582 35443 9

Set in Monophoto Univers

Printed in Great Britain
by Richard Clay (The Chaucer Press) Limited,
Bungay, Suffolk

Acknowledgement

We are grateful to the following for permission to reproduce photographs on the cover:
Picturepoint (left and centre); J. Allan Cash (right).

Contents

Questions

Answers

Preface

This workbook is designed primarily to complement *Macroeconomics: an Introduction* and covers topics in the same sequence as the textbook. It will, however, serve perfectly well as an independent study guide. It provides an extensive and comprehensive coverage of the syllabus requirements of the A Level examination boards. It will also be helpful to students taking examinations in economics set by a number of professional bodies and it should be particularly useful to first year university students.

Each chapter of the workbook follows the same pattern: an introduction which summarises the concepts used in the chapter is followed by a series of questions (short-answer, multiple choice, true–false and data response questions). Answers to all the questions are provided, and where appropriate these are given in considerable detail.

The questions range in difficulty from the relatively simple straightforward tests of factual knowledge to much more demanding checks on the ability to use analysis, to interpret data and to appreciate relationships between cause and effect.

The main aim of the book is to test and improve the student's knowledge of macroeconomics by providing material which will stimulate interest and develop understanding. To this end a large proportion of the questions are concerned with 'real world' economic problems, with particular emphasis on those of the United Kingdom.

Questions

Part 1

The national income accounts

The main function of the national income accounts is to provide comprehensive information on national income, output and expenditure. This information is necessary for purposes of economic analysis, policy making and economic forecasting.

Gross National Product and Gross Domestic Product

In the UK the principal official measurement of total output is the *Gross National Product* (GNP). This is *not* the value of the output produced within the UK. The total product of all the resources located within the UK is the *Gross Domestic Product* (GDP). The difference between these aggregates derives from the different ownership of resources. Some of the resources producing output within the UK are owned by overseas residents and some of the income earned by these assets (e.g. interest and profits) is taken out of the country by the foreign owners. This outflow of factor income is defined as *property income paid abroad*. On the other hand, UK residents own assets located overseas so that there is an inward flow of interest and profits. This inflow of income is defined as *property income from abroad*. The difference between these flows of property income is added to GDP in order to obtain GNP. Thus

GDP + Net property income from abroad = GNP

Briefly, then, GNP is the output from resources owned by residents of the country, wherever these resources happen to be located. GDP is the output from resources located in the country wherever their owners happen to live. It is important to remember that production is a continuous process so that what is being measured is a *flow of output over time* (normally one year).

National income

The total product of a country can be divided into two sorts of goods and services.

1 Goods and services which are produced and sold for consumption purposes.

2 Investment goods, consisting of the capital goods produced during the year. Any output that is added to stocks of semi-finished and finished goods during the year is also classified as investment.

This distinction is useful because the national product may be expressed in gross or net terms.

Gross National Product, as already explained, consists of the value of the total output of consumption goods and services plus investment. Some part of the output of capital goods, however, does not add to the national stock of assets. It is required to make good the plant, equipment, buildings, etc., which have become worn-out or obsolete during the course of the year. The extent to which capital is 'used up' or 'consumed' in this manner is described as *depreciation*. The total output of capital goods is described as *gross investment*, while the annual addition to the nation's stock of capital is defined as *net investment*. Hence

Gross investment – Depreciation = Net investment and
Net National Product = Gross National Product – Depreciation

Net National Product, therefore, consists of the goods and services becoming available for consumption plus any net additions to the stock of capital. Net National Product is more generally known as *national income*.

Output ≡ Income ≡ Expenditure

An understanding of this identity is essential to an understanding of how and why the national income can be measured in three different ways.

1 The output approach measures the national income by adding up the money values of the goods and services produced by the national resources during the course of the year. There are two ways of arriving at this total: (i) by adding the *final values* of the goods and services produced, and (ii) by summing the *values added* at each stage of production. If the gross values of the outputs of all enterprises were aggregated, serious problems of double counting would arise.

2 The income approach is based on the fact that the value of goods and services produced must be equal to the total (gross) payments made to factors of production for services rendered in producing the national output. The income received by factors of production divides into income from employment, income from self-employment, interest, rent and profits. These are incomes *earned* in the process of production and must be distinguished from *transfer payments* (e.g. social security benefits) which are not payments for services rendered. By restricting the definition of 'income' to mean 'factor income' we can say that national output is equal to national income.

3 The expenditure approach takes account of the fact that whatever is produced must either be sold or added to stocks. It is assumed that when a firm is adding part of the national output to its stocks, it is, in fact, buying the goods. National expenditure, therefore, is defined in such a way that it covers both that part of the national output which is sold in the market and that part which is added to stocks. It must, therefore, be equal to the national output which, as explained earlier, is equal to national income.

Personal income

The sum of all factor incomes is not the same thing as gross personal income. Some part of factor income does not accrue to persons since it is held by firms in the form of retained profits or by public bodies in the form of trading surpluses. Personal income also includes a substantial element of transfer payments (e.g. unemployment benefit and child benefit).

Gross personal income = Income from employment and self-employment + Personal receipts of rent, interest and profit + Transfer payments

Personal disposable income = Gross personal income − Direct taxes (including national insurance contributions)

Short answer questions

1 Explain why it is necessary to distinguish between Gross National Product at market prices and Gross National Product at factor cost.
2 What is meant by transfer payments and why it is necessary to distinguish them from other government expenditures for purposes of national income accounting?
3 What additions and/or subtractions must be made to total personal disposable income in order to arrive at national income?
4 Why might Gross National Product be greater than or less than Gross Domestic Product?
5 What items must be added to and/or subtracted from total domestic expenditure in order to arrive at national income?
6 What is meant by 'net property income from abroad' and why is it included in the national income calculations?
7 Explain why, over any given period of time, net investment might be negative while gross investment over the same time period is positive.
8 Why is a residual error included in the national income accounts?
9 While it is possible to measure *nominal* Gross National Product for any given year, we can only measure the extent of *changes* in the *real* GNP over a period of time. Explain why this is so.
10 Which of the following are directly *included* in the national income?
a an increase in building society deposits
b an MP's salary
c social security payments

d rents on houses owned by local authorities
e the commissions earned by estate agents for selling second-hand houses
f the profits of nationalised industries
g the profits of gambling casinos
h dividends paid on ordinary shares in UK companies
i a pension received by a UK resident from a foreign government
j the income earned by the BBC from the sale of a TV serial to foreign television companies

11 Why does the consumption of domestically produced consumer goods appear as a positive item in the national income accounts while the consumption of capital goods appears as a negative item?

12 Why is an estimate of the annual rental value of owner-occupied houses included in the national income accounts?

13 If a firm misjudges the market conditions and has to sell some of its output at a loss (i.e. less than the cost of production), how can the value of output be equal to total factor income?

14 One major problem in national income accounting is the need to avoid *double counting.* Explain what is meant by this term and how the problem can be overcome.

15 The table below gives hypothetical values of items in the national income accounts of a particular country. Expenditures are measured at market prices.

	£ million
Consumers' expenditure	135 000
General government final consumption	50 000
Gross domestic fixed capital formation	25 000
Value of physical increase in stocks and work in progress	−2 000
Exports of goods and services	45 000
Imports of goods and services	40 000
Net property income from abroad	−50
Taxes on expenditure	60 000
Subsidies	10 000
Capital consumption	30 000

Calculate
a Total Domestic Expenditure at market prices.
b Total Final Expenditure at market prices.
c Gross Domestic Product at market prices.
d Gross National Product at market prices.
e Gross National Product at factor cost.
f National Income.

16 'Terms such as the *black economy* or *hidden economy* are used to refer to these concealed transactions.' To which type of transaction does this quotation refer?

17 Is it possible to estimate the size of the black or hidden economy, and does its existence seriously limit the use of the national income statistics?

18 From the figures given below, calculate the percentage change in the real national income over the ten-year period.

	Year 1	**Year 10**
National income (£ million)	50 000	75 000
Index of prices	100	125

19 The table below contains a random selection of items from the national accounts of a country which has a government sector but does not engage in international trade. It gives sufficient information to calculate the national income by one of the traditional methods.

Net investment	200
Personal tax payments	80
Personal savings	100
Consumers' expenditure	800
Depreciation	100
Government spending on goods and services	150
Government spending on social security benefits	75
Taxes on expenditure	70
Subsidies	20

Calculate
a GNP at market prices.
b national income.

Multiple choice questions

20 The total value of all incomes *earned* by UK residents is equal to

A national income.
B personal disposable income.
C GNP at factor cost.
D GDP at factor cost.

21 The difference between Gross National Product at factor cost and national income is

A net property income from abroad.
B capital consumption.
C transfer payments.
D taxes and subsidies.

22 An unemployed worker receiving £2000 per annum in supplementary benefits decided to start his own business using savings accumulated when he was in work. He employed his wife (who was previously not in paid employment) part-time, and paid her a salary of £3000 per annum. During the first year, the business made a gross trading profit of £12 000 but incurred depreciation on assets of £1000. As a result of these activities the national income increased by

A £15 000
B £14 000
C £12 000
D £10 000
E £8 000

23 In order to change Gross Domestic Product to Gross National Product, allowance has to be made for
1 depreciation.
2 expenditure on imports and earnings from exports.
3 net property income from abroad.

A 1, 2, and 3
B 1 and 2 only
C 2 and 3 only
D 1 only
E 3 only

24 If the following accounting procedures were applied to the car manufacturing industry, which of them would involve some element of double counting? The items refer to events during the course of one year.
1 adding the value of the cars sold to the value of the increase in the stocks of unsold cars
2 adding the value of the changes in the stocks of unsold cars to the value of the changes in the stocks of car components
3 adding the total value of the output of cars to the total value of the output of car components

A 1, 2 and 3
B 1 and 2 only
C 2 and 3 only
D 1 only
E 3 only

25 Retailers bought bread from bakers for £100 million and sold it to the public for £150 million. The bakers bought the flour from millers for £80 million and the millers paid the farmers £50 million for the wheat. The total contribution of these activities to the national income was

A £380 million
B £280 million
C £230 million
D £150 million

26 Which of the following is/are correct?

1 Gross National Product minus Gross Domestic Product equals net property income from abroad.
2 National income plus depreciation equals Gross National Product.
3 Gross factor income plus transfer payments equals personal disposable income.

A 1, 2 and 3
B 1 and 2 only
C 2 and 3 only
D 1 only
E 3 only

Questions **27**, **28** and **29** are based on the following table.

	£ million
Total domestic expenditure	40 000
Balance of exports over imports	+4 000
Net property income from abroad	+3 000
Taxes on expenditure	1 000
Subsidies	500
Capital consumption	1 000

27 Gross Domestic Product at market prices is equal to

A £40 000 million
B £44 000 million
C £47 000 million
D £48 000 million

28 Gross National Product at market prices is equal to

A £45 000 million
B £45 500 million
C £47 000 million
D £47 500 million

29 National income is equal to

A £45 000 million
B £45 500 million
C £46 500 million
D £47 000 million

True or false?

30 **a** The total value of final output equals the sum of the values added at each stage of production.

b Gross personal income plus transfer payments equals personal disposable income.

c Transfer incomes can be identified because they are incomes which are not subject to tax.

d It is difficult to obtain any reliable estimate of GNP in a subsistence economy.

e It is possible for GNP to be increasing while the average productivity of the labour force is decreasing.

f Changes in real GNP per capita are widely used as indicators of changes in living standards.

g National income is equal to the sum of all personal incomes received during the course of one year.

h The inclusion of the salaries of civil servants in the national income would amount to double counting since these incomes are paid from tax revenues and these taxes have already been counted as part of other people's incomes.

i If the nominal GNP of a country is increasing, then the average standard of living must also be increasing.

Data response questions

31 This question is based on the table opposite, which contains information extracted from the national income accounts of the United Kingdom.

a Calculate the missing values at (i), (ii) and (iii) for the year 1978.

b What is the significance of the word *physical* in the heading 'Value of physical increase in stocks and work in progress'?

c What additional information is required in order to calculate the real change in Gross Domestic Product over the period covered by the table?

d What was the value of total domestic investment in 1981?

e Why do you think there was a fall in both fixed investment and in the level of stocks held in 1981 compared with 1980?

Expenditure on the gross domestic product (£ million at current prices)

	Gross domestic product		**Final expenditure on goods and services at market prices**								
	At market prices	At factor cost	Total	Consumers' expenditure	General Government consumption	Gross domestic fixed capital formation	Value of physical increase in stocks and work in progress	Exports of goods and services	Imports of goods and services	Taxes on expenditure	Subsidies
1975	104 760	94 339	133 771	64 652	22 950	20 408	−1436	27 197	29 011	14 111	3690
1976	124 546	111 566	161 462	74 850	26 739	23 556	881	35 436	36 916	16 456	3476
1977	143 775	127 050	186 382	85 948	29 244	25 727	1881	43 582	42 607	20 028	3303
1978	165 375	(i)	(ii)	98 867	32 984	29 743	1601	(iii)	45 546	22 951	3655
1979	193 368	167 937	247 984	117 071	38 324	34 469	2995	55 123	54 616	29 868	4437
1980	226 112	194 538	284 025	135 738	48 424	39 411	−2706	63 158	57 913	36 882	5308
1981	248 537	211 411	309 267	151 286	54 942	39 377	−4160	67 822	60 730	42 989	5863

Source: *Economic Trends*, HMSO, January 1983

32 This question is based on the graph opposite, which refers to the UK economy.

a Explain what is meant by 'Gross Domestic Product at constant factor cost'.

b To what extent does the information contained in the graph imply that the average standard of living in the UK fell over the period 1979–82?

33 This question is based on the following details of a country's economic activities during the course of one year.

	£ million
New buildings produced	100
New plant and machinery produced	90
Consumer goods produced	150
Depreciation of buildings	10
Depreciation of plant and machinery	9
Stocks of consumer goods at beginning of year	30
Stocks of consumer goods at end of year	50
Exports of capital goods	30
Exports of consumer goods	30
Imports of capital goods	10
Imports of consumer goods	50

In the economy for this particular year,

a what was the value of gross investment?

b what was the value of total consumption?

c what was the value of GNP?

d what was the value of national income?

Show clearly how you arrive at your answers.

Gross Domestic Product at constant factor cost, based on output data (1975 = 100)

*Preliminary estimate

Source: *Economic Progress Report*, HMSO, 16th June 1982

Part 2

Consumption, saving and investment

Consumption

In the macro sense, consumption is defined as that part of the national output which is used up in the course of some accounting period, usually one year.

Consumers' expenditure represents consumption by private individuals (households) and constitutes the major part of total expenditure in the UK. When consumers' expenditure is plotted against income, a *consumption function* is obtained which shows the levels of consumption at different levels of income. Since consumer spending is determined largely by *disposable* income (income after adjustments for tax and transfer payments) it is sometimes the practice to plot consumption against disposable income rather than total income.

Saving

In a simple two-sector economy, that is, one with only households and firms, the difference between income and consumption is saving. Thus, saving is that part of income which is not spent. In an economy with a government sector (i.e. where taxes are applied to income), saving represents the difference between disposable income and consumers' expenditure. When saving is plotted against income, a *savings function* is obtained showing the amounts of saving at different levels of income. Again, we find that saving is sometimes plotted against disposable income rather than total income.

Investment

Investment is defined as the creation of capital goods. It includes the construction of buildings, the manufacture of machinery and additions to stocks of raw materials, semi-finished goods and finished goods. Total investment also includes any additions to claims on the output of other countries (i.e. any net additions to overseas assets). When investment is plotted against income we have the *investment function*, which shows the changes in investment as income changes.

Notation

The following conventional abbreviations are used in some of the questions in this section of the book.

Y = total income
Y_d = disposable income
C = consumption
S = saving
I = investment
APC = average propensity to consume
MPC = marginal propensity to consume
APS = average propensity to save
MPS = marginal propensity to save
Δ = 'a very small change in', e.g. ΔC = a very small change in C

Short answer questions

1 This question refers to the graph below.

a In the graph, which consumption function may be represented by an expression of the form

$C = a + bY$?

b Which consumption function shows positive saving at all levels of income?

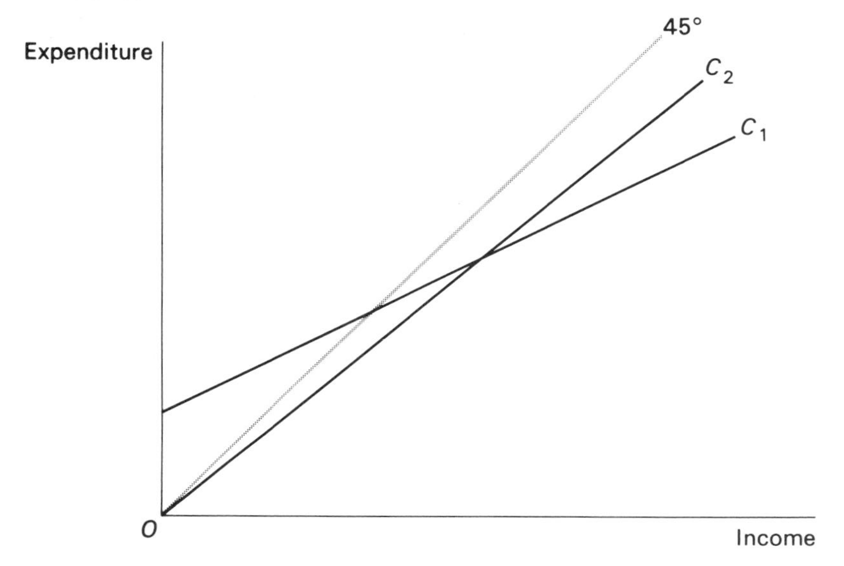

Note: Both axes are drawn to the same scale.

2 What are the main factors determining the aggregate level of consumer spending in an economy?

3 Why does the MPC fall continuously as income rises?

4 The marginal propensity to consume of an economy is greater than . . . but less than . . . for all levels of income. What are the missing words?

5 Explain why the MPC can never be negative.

6 A consumption function is often expressed in the form

$$C = a + bY_d$$

Explain the use of the terms a and b.

7 In an economy consisting of only households and firms, why must the sum of the MPC and the MPS always equal 1?

8 'A consumption function which shows how consumers' expenditure changes as income changes is based on the assumption that other things remain equal.' To what 'other things' does this statement refer?

9 'A relatively large amount of personal saving is contractual.' Explain what this means and give two examples of contractual saving.

10 Why is the level of total saving likely to be fairly unresponsive to changes in the rate of interest?

11 At relatively low levels of income, current consumption is likely to exceed current income. How can this be so, and what term is used to describe what is taking place?

12 The table below shows the different amounts of consumer spending associated with different levels of income.

Income (£ million)	Consumers' expenditure (£ million)
1000	1500
2000	2400
3000	3150
4000	3600
5000	4000
6000	4200

Use this information to obtain values at each level of income for

a APC

b MPC

c total saving

d APS

e MPS

13 Assume that $Y_d = 0.8Y$, and that APC out of disposable income is $C = 0.75Y_d$ and this proportion is constant. Now assume that as a result of an increase in income tax, disposable income is reduced to $Y_d = 0.6Y$. What happens to consumption as a proportion of total income?

14 This question refers to the graph below.

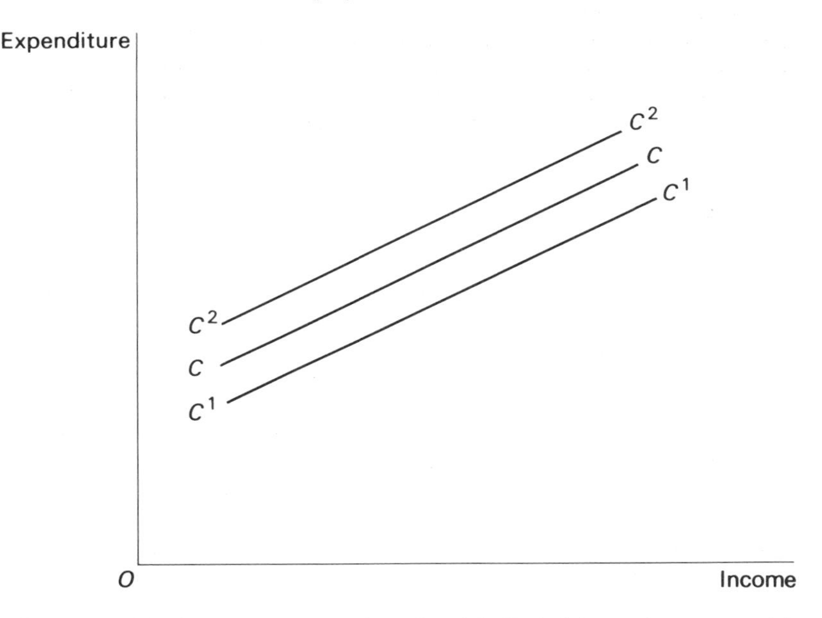

Starting with the consumption function labelled C in each case, explain whether the following changes would be more likely to lead to a movement of the consumption function to C^1 or to C^2.

a an increase in disposable income
b an increase in the rate of interest charged on hire purchase agreements
c a strong expectation that prices will fall in the future
d a reduction in the inequality of income distribution

15 What is meant by 'the present value of future earnings'?

16 a What is meant by the term 'the marginal efficiency of capital'?
b Why does the marginal efficiency of capital tend to fall as the volume of investment increases?

17 An industry uses machines which each produce 200 units of a consumer good per annum. Its capital stock, at present, is fully utilised. The machines have a life of ten years and the capital stock has been built up evenly over time. We assume there is no technical progress.

	Demand for product (units)	**Number of machines**				
		Existing stock	**Required stock**	**Replacement demand**	**Net investment**	**Total investment**
Year 1	10 000	50	50	5	0	5
Year 2	12 000	50				

The industry experiences a 20 per cent increase in the demand for its product in year 2. Complete the preceding table and explain how this simple arithmetical example illustrates the principle of the accelerator.

18 'Economic theory uses very neat and precise formulae for calculating the net returns on a proposed investment project. These calculations may be carried out with great accuracy but the investment decision will still be based largely on intelligent guesswork.' Explain.

Multiple choice questions

19 When the distribution of income in an economy is very unequal, a more equal distribution of income is likely to lead to

A a fall in APS and a fall in MPS.
B a rise in APS and a rise in MPS.
C a fall in APS and a rise in MPS.
D a rise in APS and a fall in MPS.

20 In the graph below, *CC* represents an aggregate consumption function.

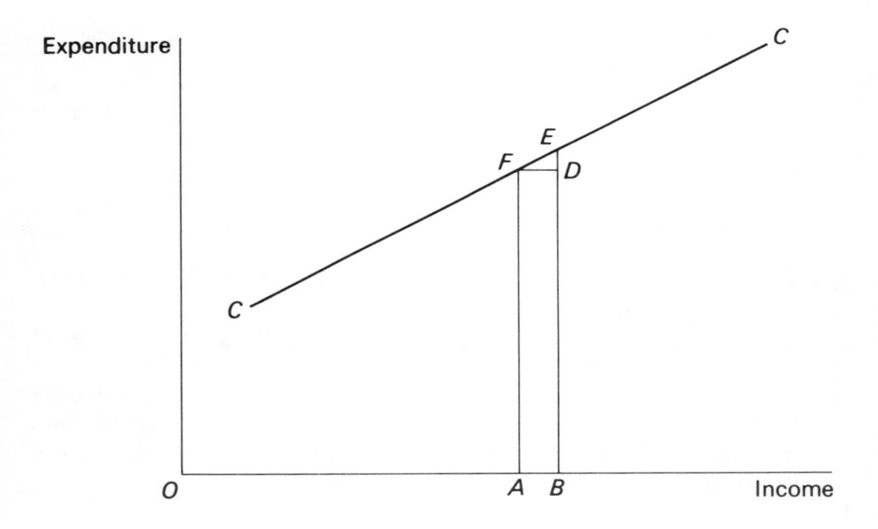

The MPC at all levels of income is equal to

A *ED*

B $\frac{EB}{OB}$

C $\frac{FD}{ED}$

D $\frac{ED}{AB}$

21 In a two-sector economy, which of the following defines the MPS?

A $\Delta Y - \Delta C$

B $Y - C$

C $\frac{\Delta Y - \Delta C}{\Delta Y}$

D $\frac{S}{Y}$

22 In a two-sector economy, which of the following defines the APS?

A $\frac{Y}{S}$

B $\frac{\Delta S}{Y}$

C $\frac{Y - C}{Y}$

D $\frac{\Delta S}{\Delta Y}$

23 Which of the following would *not* represent an increase in net investment?
1 an increase in building society deposits
2 increased expenditure on repairs to the motorway network
3 an increase in stocks of unfinished goods

A 1, 2, and 3
B 1 and 2 only
C 2 and 3 only
D 1 only
E 3 only

24 All other things remaining equal, which of the following would *cause* an increase in the marginal efficiency of capital?
1 an increase in the rate of saving
2 a reduction in the rate of interest
3 an increase in the productivity of capital

A 1, 2, and 3
B 1 and 2 only
C 2 and 3 only
D 1 only
E 3 only

True or false?

25 **a** Other things remaining equal, as income rises the APS falls.
b In a two-sector economy (i.e. only households and firms), given the level of income and the APS, we can calculate the aggregate level of consumption.
c Where the consumption function is drawn as a straight line that intersects the expenditure axis at a point other than the origin, the APS will be constant.
d If the MPC is falling as income rises, then APC must also be falling.
e The accelerator principle indicates that a change in consumption will tend to lead to a more than proportionate change in the rate of investment.
f If an industry has a capital–output ratio of 2, it means that £1000 worth of capital can produce £2000 worth of output per annum.
g If the consumption function is a straight line passing through the origin, APS equals MPS at all levels of income.
h Apart from his or her current income, it is likely that a person's propensity to consume is influenced by the accumulated capital wealth possessed by that person.

Data response questions

26 A firm is considering the purchase of a machine, the purchase price of which is £5000. The life expectancy of the machine is five years, and after all costs, including depreciation, have been met, the net returns on the machine are expected to be:

Year 1	Year 2	Year 3	Year 4	Year 5
£1500	£1450	£1350	£1150	£900

a If the rate of interest over the five-year period is assumed to be 5 per cent, what is the present value of this expected future stream of earnings?
b What conclusions can be drawn about the expected profitability of this investment project?
c How would an increase in the rate of interest to 10 per cent affect the firm's decision on whether or not to purchase the machine?

27 This question is based on the following diagram.

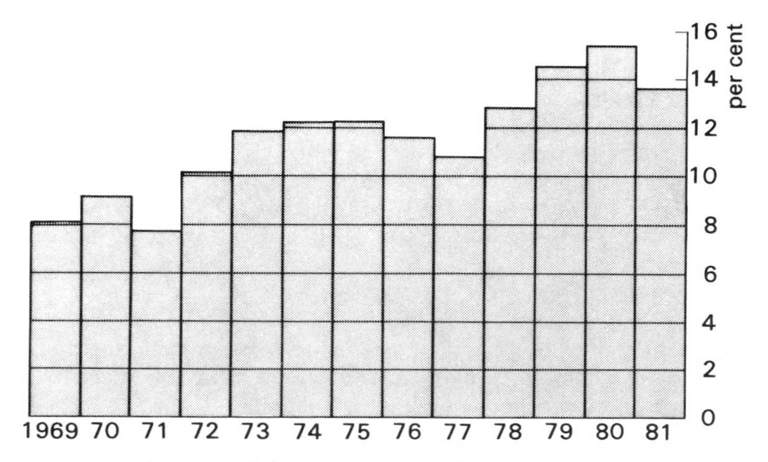

Personal saving ratio, UK (percentages of personal disposable income)

Source: Prest and Coppock, *The UK Economy*, 9th edition, Weidenfeld and Nicolson

a What is meant by total personal saving and what are the main forms of this type of saving?
b Given the fact that the 1970s was a period of relatively high rates of inflation and rising unemployment, how would you account for the significant increase in the personal savings ratio (from 8 per cent to about 14 per cent)?

Part 3
The determination of income

1 The two-sector economy

The circular flow of income

A most useful concept in the theory of income determination is that of the circular flow of income. In a two-sector economy with only households and firms, the model of the circular flow is very simple.

In order to produce goods and services, firms buy the services of labour, capital, land and entrepreneurship from households. In return for these services, members of households receive income in the form of wages, interest, rent and

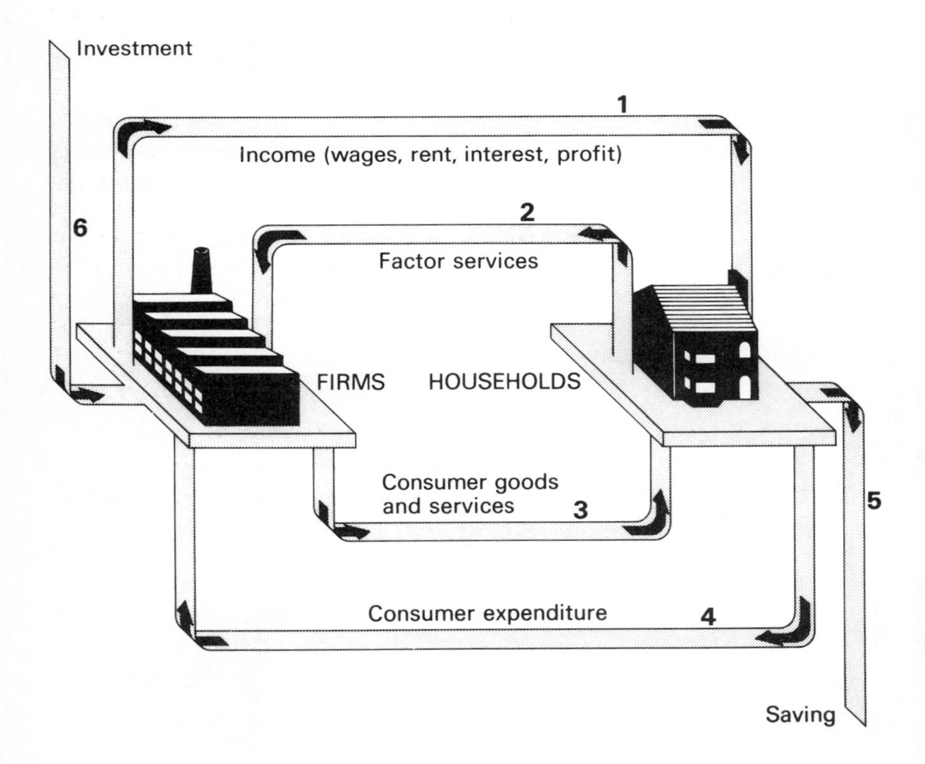

profit. These two 'flows' are shown in the diagram on page 22 where flow **2** represents a *real* flow and flow **1** a *money* flow. The consumer goods and services produced by firms are purchased by households and these transactions are shown as a real flow (**3**) and a money flow (**4**). Households, however, do not spend all their income; some is saved and hence is withdrawn from the circular flow of income. *Saving is a leakage or withdrawal from the circular flow of income* (**5**). In addition to households' demands for consumption goods and services, firms also receive demands for capital goods (i.e. investment) from other firms. This demand arises outside the circular flow so that *investment is an injection into the circular flow of income* (**6**).

Saving and investment

In macroeconomics, it is important to distinguish between what firms and households *plan* or intend to do and what is actually achieved (i.e. *realised*). The amount which firms plan to invest during a particular time period will not necessarily be equal to the amount of investment actually carried out during that time period. Remember that investment includes additions to stocks so that, if total demand is greater than or less than firms anticipate, there will be some *unplanned* changes in stocks. These unplanned changes in investment will mean that realised investment will not be equal to planned investment. In other words,

$$\text{Planned investment} \gtrless \text{Realised investment}$$

This particular distinction is important because firms will react to unplanned changes in their stocks by changing their levels of output. It must be noted that flow **6** in the diagram refers to planned investment.

The link between saving and investment is important because while saving makes investment possible it does not cause investment to take place. In general, saving and investment are carried out by different groups of people acting for quite different reasons. There can be no assurance, therefore, that the amounts which the community desires to save will be equal to the amounts which firms desire to invest. Thus

$$\text{Planned investment} \gtrless \text{Planned saving}$$

There is, however, one sense in which saving and investment are always equal! If saving is defined as that part of income which is not spent (i.e. realised saving), then

$$Y = C + S$$

If investment is defined as that part of output which is not consumed (i.e. realised investment) then

$$\text{Output } (Y) = C + I$$

These two equations give us the identity

Realised investment ≡ Realised saving

Any discrepancy between planned saving and planned investment leads to unplanned changes in stocks which bring about the equality set out above.

Equilibrium

An equilibrium level of income exists when no forces are tending to change the level of planned output. Income is stable. National income and output will be in equilibrium, therefore, when aggregate demand is equal to the value of current production (i.e. aggregate supply). Since income (Y) is equal to output, aggregate production is equal to flow **1** in the diagram on page 22. Aggregate demand consists of flow **4** (i.e. planned C) *plus* flow **6** (i.e. planned I). Hence the condition for equilibrium is

$$Y = C + I$$

If $Y > C + I$, firms will find that stocks are accumulating (unplanned I) and they will react by reducing output; income will fall.

If $Y < C + I$, firms will find that stocks are running down (unplanned disinvestment) and they will react by increasing production; income will rise.

The equilibrium condition can also be expressed in terms of saving and investment as follows.

Aggregate demand = Planned consumption + Planned investment
Aggregate income (= Output) = Planned consumption + Planned saving

Clearly, therefore, aggregate demand will only be equal to the value of output if

Planned I = Planned S

or, in more general terms, if

Planned injections = Planned leakages

The multiplier

The equilibrium level of income will probably not be attained. In the real world it is better to regard it as the level of income to which, in the absence of external disturbances, economic forces will tend to move an economy. In a two-sector economy, the external disturbance which tends to shift the equilibrium level of income is a change in the rate of investment.

Changes in the rate of production of capital goods will cause changes in income, but the relationship between a change in investment and the subsequent change in income is not a simple one.

An increase in I will lead to a change in Y which is much greater than the initial change in I. Similarly, a fall in I will cause Y to fall by an amount greater than the initial fall in I. The key to the relationship between ΔI and ΔY is the *multiplier*, the numerical value of which is $\Delta Y/\Delta I$. Thus, if an increase in the rate of investment of £10 million leads to a subsequent increase in income of £30 million, the multiplier is 3.

The size of the multiplier depends upon the proportion of any change in income which is passed on within the circular flow. In other words, it depends upon the size of the community's MPC. For example, if an increase in investment leads to an immediate increase in income of £10 million and the community's MPC is 0.6, then the increase in income will lead to additional spending of £600 000. This spending will cause a further rise in income of £600 000, of which six-tenths will be spent. The process will go on until the increments in income become infinitesimally small. Income will carry on increasing, in fact, until planned saving is once again equal to planned investment.

$$\text{The multiplier} = \frac{1}{1-\text{MPC}} = \frac{1}{\text{MPS}}$$

Short answer questions

1 What circumstances would lead to
 a realised investment exceeding planned investment?
 b planned investment exceeding realised investment?

2 What is meant by an equilibrium level of income and what are the necessary conditions for equilibrium in a two-sector economy?

3 'Since saving is always equal to investment, an increase in saving must lead to an increase in investment.' Comment on this statement.

4 Explain why, if other things remain equal, an increase in planned saving is likely to lead to a fall in realised savings.

5 This question is based on the diagram below.

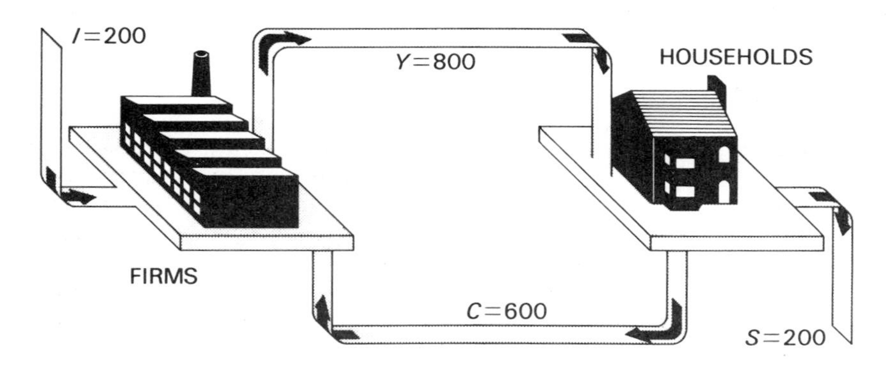

Assuming that APC remains constant and the rate of investment increases to 250, what will be the values of

a Y
b C
c S
when the new equilibrium level of income is established?

6 This question is based on the following table which shows how consumption changes as the level of income changes.

Income (£ million)	Consumption (£ million)
1000	1500
2000	2400
3000	3150
4000	3725
5000	4000
6000	4175

Given that investment is constant at £1000 million, what is the equilibrium level of income?

7 The rate of investment in an economy increases by £5000 million and sets the multiplier process in motion. In the initial stages of this process, saving increases as follows.

£2000m. + £1200m. + £720m. + . . .

a What is the next term in the series?
b What is the eventual increase in the equilibrium level of income?

8 Explain why an increase in unplanned investment ultimately leads to a reduction in income.

9 Why does the size of the multiplier vary directly with the size of the marginal propensity to consume?

10 In an economy, investment is constant at the rate of £1500 million, and

$C = £500 \text{ million} + 0.8Y$

at all levels of income.
a What is the equilibrium level of income?
b What is the value of the multiplier?

11 If investment remains constant and consumption spending increases (i.e. there is an increase in the propensity to consume), will the level of saving be higher, lower or unchanged at the new equilibrium level of income? Explain your answer.

12 The diagram on page 27 shows the first few 'rounds' of the multiplier process following an increase in the rate of investment of £1000 million. The MPC of the community is constant. The question applies to a two-sector economy.
a What increase in saving will take place in round 3?
b What is the value of the multiplier?

13 'When an individual increases his saving, he increases his wealth. When a community tries to increase its rate of saving, it might well find itself, eventually, with a *lower* level of total saving.' Explain.

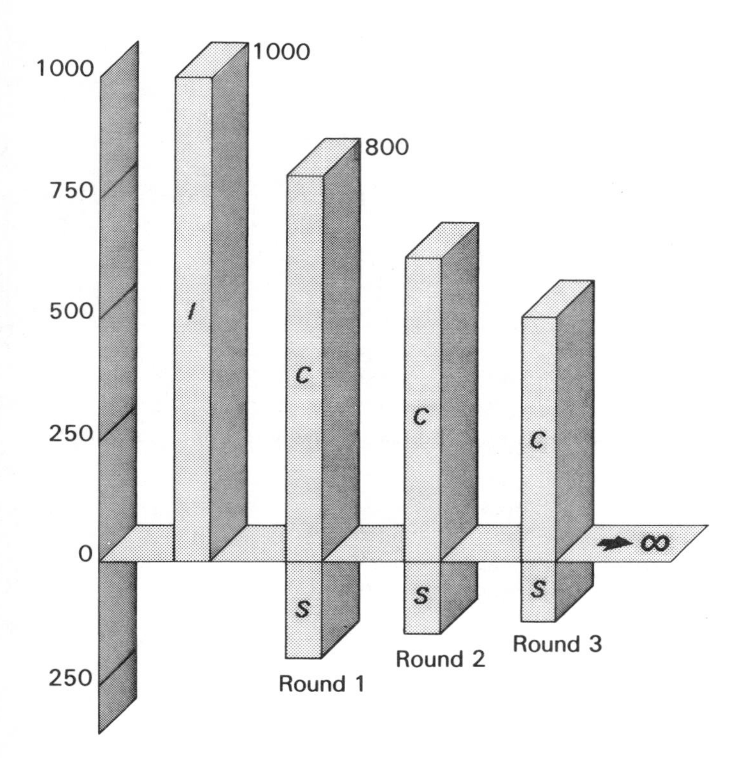

Multiple choice questions

14 If the community plans to save more than firms plan to invest and the amount which firms *plan to invest* remains constant, then
1 the eventual outcome will be an increase in total saving.
2 the immediate effect will be an increase in investment.
3 the eventual outcome will be a fall in income.

A 1, 2, and 3
B 1 and 2 only
C 2 and 3 only
D 1 only
E 3 only

15 In order to calculate the multiplier it is necessary to know
1 the proportion of total income which is saved.
2 the proportion of saving which is invested.
3 the proportion of an increase in income which is spent.

A 1, 2, and 3
B 1 and 2 only
C 2 and 3 only
D 1 only
E 3 only

16 If the rate of investment in an economy rises by £1000 million at all levels of income and the MPC is constant at 0.75, national income will increase by

A £1250 million
B £1750 million
C £2000 million
D £4000 million
E £7500 million

17 Which of the following would tend to *reduce* the size of the multiplier?

A a fall in the rate of investment
B a fall in the level of national income
C a fall in the rate of saving
D an increase in the rate of saving
E an increase in the propensity to consume

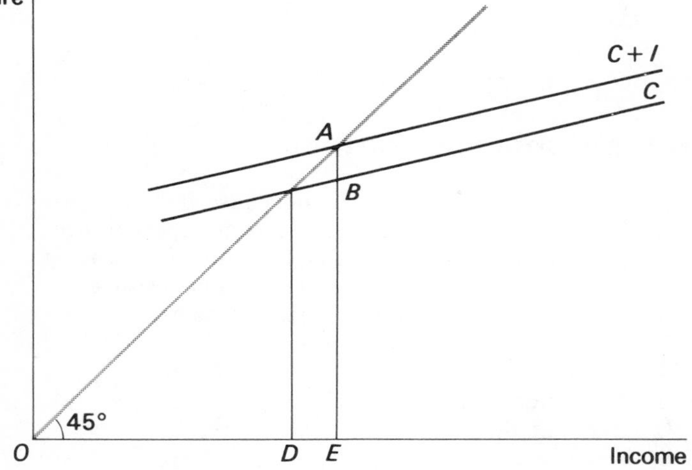

Note: Both axes are drawn to the same scale.

18 In the graph above, the value of the multiplier is equal to

A $\frac{DE}{AB}$

B $\frac{AE}{DE}$

C $\frac{AB}{OE}$

D $\frac{AE}{OE}$

19 In an economy with a constant MPC, an increase in investment at all levels of income will lead to an increase in

1 savings.
2 consumption.
3 national income.

A 1, 2, and 3
B 1 and 2 only
C 2 and 3 only
D 1 only
E 3 only

20 If an increase in investment of £1000 million causes income to increase from £20 000 million to £24 000 million, we can deduce that the MPS is

A 0.25
B 0.4
C 0.5
D 0.75

Questions **21** and **22** are based on the graph below.

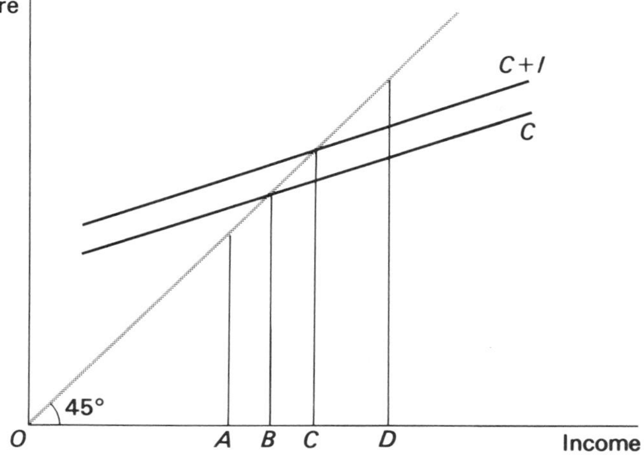

Note: Both axes are drawn to the same scale.

21 At which level of income is planned S greater than planned I?

A OA
B OB
C OC
D OD

22 At which level of income is planned S equal to planned I?

A OA
B OB
C OC
D OD

23 Which of the following expressions represents the multiplier?

A $\dfrac{1}{\left(\dfrac{\Delta S}{S}\right)}$

B $\dfrac{1}{1-\Delta C}$

C $\dfrac{1}{\Delta Y-\Delta S}$

D $\dfrac{1}{\left(\dfrac{\Delta Y-\Delta C}{\Delta Y}\right)}$

True or false?

24 **a** If realised saving and realised investment are equal, then planned saving and planned investment must also be equal.
b If the MPS falls, the value of the multiplier will increase.
c The economy is always in equilibrium when realised income is equal to realised expenditure.
d A more equal distribution of income will lead to an increase in the size of the multiplier.
e A downward multiplier process comes into play whenever (i) there is an increase in the rate of withdrawals or (ii) there is a fall in the rate of injection.
f Investment comprises that part of total output which is not consumed.
g Whatever is saved by households is borrowed by firms and used to finance investment. Saving, therefore, is always equal to investment.

Data response questions

25

	Income	Consumption	Saving	Planned investment	Unplanned investment	Realised investment
Period 1	2000	1700	300	300	0	300
Period 2						
Period 3						
Period *N*						

The table above shows an economy in equilibrium in period 1. Initially (i.e. in period 1), the consumption function is

$$C = 100 + 0.8Y$$

In period 2, the MPC falls to $0.75Y$ and remains constant at this value. Planned investment also remains constant at 300. Complete the table, showing the changes in the variables for the subsequent time periods (periods 2 and 3) and the final equilibrium values (period *N*). Assume that consumption responds immediately to any change in income and that firms adjust output in the period following a change in demand.

26 In a particular economy, firms spend £200 million per time period on investment (at all levels of income). Total saving is equal to $-600 + 0.2Y$.
a Construct a graph, labelling one axis 'Saving and investment' and the other axis 'Income'. Plot the saving and investment functions for values of income from 0 to £5000 million and label them '*S*' and '*I*'. Use the graph to obtain the equilibrium level of income.
b What is the level of consumption in equilibrium?
c What is the value of the multiplier in this economy?
d Now assume that the level of investment increases by 50 per cent at all levels of income and, at the same time, the MPS increases by 25 per cent at all levels of income. Construct a new graph plotting expenditure against income. Use the same scale on both axes so that a line drawn through the origin at 45° traces out all the points at which income is equal to expenditure. Plot (i) the consumption function and (ii) the consumption and investment function for all values of income from 0 to £5000 million. Obtain the new equilibrium level of income and verify your answer arithmetically.

2 The three-sector economy

The government sector

This section of the book extends the model of the circular flow of income by introducing a government sector, but this does not alter the basic analysis. It simply means that the model must be modified to allow for an additional injection in the form of government spending (G) and an additional leakage in the form of taxation (T).

Since we are dealing with the determination of output and income, it is important to remember that the variable G represents only the government's demands for goods and services. It does not include transfer payments which, *in themselves*, do not represent a demand for output.

Equilibrium

The fundamental requirement for an equilibrium level of income and output remains unchanged, that is, it is necessary for aggregate demand to be equal to the value of the output produced, which means that planned injections should be equal to planned leakages. The components of these variables, however, have to be increased in number to take account of G and T. We can now say that national income will be in equilibrium when

(i) Aggregate demand = Output (= Income)
i.e. $C + I + G = Y$

(ii) Planned injections = Planned leakages
i.e. when $I + G = S + T$

It is important to note that it is a relationship between *total* planned injections and *total* planned leakages which affects the level of income. In a three-sector economy, equilibrium does *not* require that $S = T$ or that $G = T$. In fact it is very unlikely that a government will aim to equate G and T. It is much more likely to aim at a Budget deficit (i.e. $G > T$) or a Budget surplus (i.e. $G < T$) depending upon the economic circumstances and its particular policy objectives. A Budget deficit will be financed by borrowing and the national debt represents the accumulated total of such borrowings.

The multiplier

The size of the multiplier depends upon the proportion of any increase in income which is spent. The greater the proportion spent, the greater the subsequent increase in income. In other words, the greater the leakage (or withdrawal), the smaller the multiplier effect. In a two-sector economy, the multiplier was 1/MPS. The introduction of the government sector does not alter the basic formula; the multiplier is still equal to the reciprocal of any increase in income which leaks out of the circular flow.

$$\text{The multiplier} = \frac{1}{1 - \text{MPC}} = \frac{1}{\text{MPS} + \text{MRT}}$$

where MRT is the marginal rate of taxation.

This explanation has been confined to the effects of *increased* spending. The multiplier also operates to bring about a cumulative *downward* movement in income when there is a fall in one of the autonomous components of aggregate demand.

Autonomous and induced expenditures

It is useful at this stage to distinguish between autonomous and induced expenditures. In relation to the circular flow of income, an autonomous expenditure is one which does not vary with the level of income; it is independent of changes in income. An induced expenditure is one which is determined by and hence varies with income.

In the examples in the previous section, investment was assumed to be constant (i.e. autonomous). In the real world, some investment will be autonomous (e.g. replacement investment and investment stimulated by innovations), but some will certainly be influenced by changes in income. Government spending on goods and services is generally taken to be an example of autonomous expenditure, but some part of the public spending on transfer payments will be closely related to movements in income. Tax revenues will, of course, be a function of income and vary directly as income varies.

Short answer questions

1 'If the government plans for a Budget surplus or deficit, it means that planned leakages cannot equal planned injections.' Is this a correct statement? Explain your answer.
2 When households spend income they have received in the form of transfer payments, they create a demand for goods and services. Why, then, are these transfer payments not included in G in the aggregate demand function, $C+I+G$?
3 The value of the multiplier is equal to the reciprocal of the marginal rate of . . . . Supply the missing word to form a definition of the multiplier which is applicable to all economies regardless of the number of sectors they have.
4 If all other things remain equal, why will an increase in government expenditure on goods and services of £1 000 million lead to a larger increase in income than a reduction in taxation of £1 000 million?
5 Why does a fall in the rate of taxation lead to a rise in the value of the multiplier?
6 Why are some tax revenues and social security benefits regarded as automatic stabilisers?
7 'Fiscal policy should be designed to balance the economy, not the Budget.' Why is this a generally accepted view of fiscal policy?
8 In what ways might the existence of a large public debt lead to a significant redistribution of income?

9 Parts of the national debt are referred to as *floating debt, internal debt* and *external debt*. Explain what each of these terms means.

10 This question is based on the graph below.

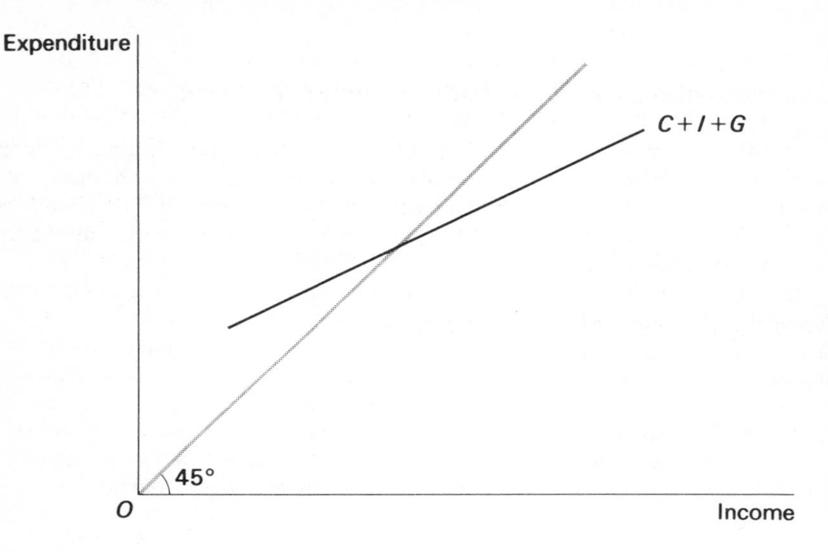

What would happen to the $C+I+G$ line if

a there was an increase in direct taxes, but no change in government spending?

b government expenditure on goods and services, and taxation were increased by equal amounts?

11 Why might a proportional indirect tax be regressive in its effects?

12 This question is based on the graph below.

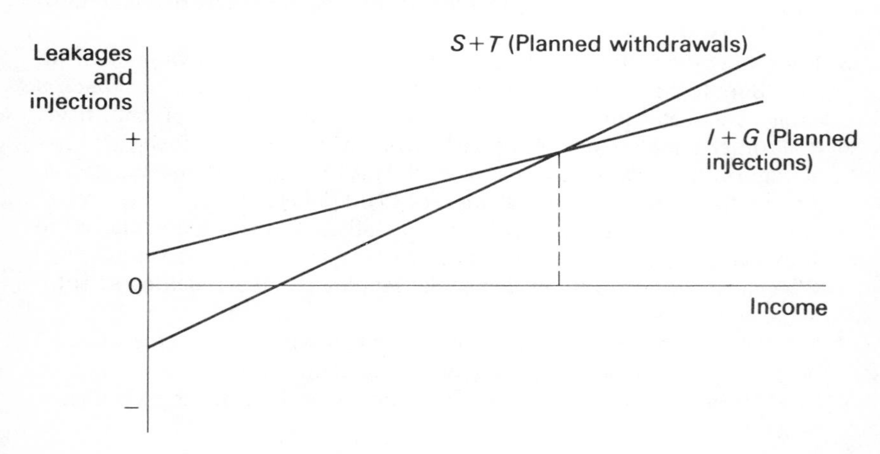

The diagram shows the leakage (withdrawal) and injection functions for a particular economy. G is an autonomous item, while I contains both autonomous and induced elements. What would happen to

a the equilibrium level of income and

b the total value of leakages $(S + T)$,

if there were a fall in the average propensity to consume?

13 In a closed economy with government, households spend four-fifths of their disposable income (at all levels of Y_d) and the marginal rate of taxation is constant at $0.25Y$. What is the value of the multiplier? Assume there are no transfer payments.

14 The construction of a motorway is financed by selling long-term fixed interest government securities to residents of the country. Does this mean that the 'true cost' of the motorway is transferred to a future generation?

Multiple choice questions

15 This question is based on the graph below.

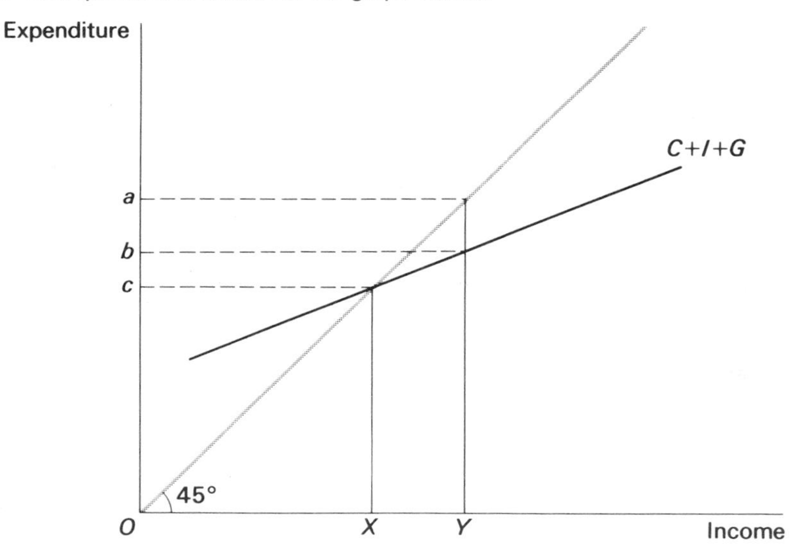

Note: Both axes are drawn to the same scale.

OY represents the full employment level of income and $C + I + G$ the existing aggregate demand function. There is a deflationary gap equal to

A *ab*
B *bc*
C *ac*
D *XY*

16 In an economy with a marginal propensity to consume of $0.8Y_d$ and a marginal rate of taxation of $0.25Y$, it is decided to raise Y by £1000 million. Other things remaining equal, it will be necessary to raise government spending on goods and services by

A £200 million
B £250 million
C £400 million
D £500 million

17 Which of the following would lead to a fall in the value of the multiplier?
1 a fall in the propensity to save
2 a fall in the rates of taxation
3 a fall in the propensity to consume

A 1, 2, and 3
B 1 and 2 only
C 2 and 3 only
D 1 only
E 3 only

18 In a closed economy with government, macroeconomic disequilibrium exists when

A government spending is not equal to tax revenue.
B planned investment is not equal to planned saving.
C national output is not equal to national income.
D aggregate output is not equal to planned spending.
E realised investment is not equal to realised saving.

19 The following table shows the planned amounts of G and I at given levels of national income in a closed economy with government.

Y	***G***	***I***
30 000	1000	3000
25 000	1000	3000
20 000	1000	3000
15 000	1000	3000
10 000	1000	3000

$$T = \frac{1}{10}Y \qquad S = \frac{1}{9}Y_d$$

In this economy, the equilibrium level of income is

A 30 000
B 25 000
C 20 000
D 15 000
E 10 000

True or false?

20 **a** A Budget or a mini-Budget is required before any changes in the rates of taxation can be carried out.
b A reduction in direct taxes and an increase in indirect taxes would make the tax system more progressive.
c A proportional income tax would leave the distribution of income unchanged.
d The UK system of taxation does not contain any form of payroll tax.
e Fiscal drag occurs when tax thresholds or personal tax allowances are not adjusted to take account of inflation.
f 'Crowding out' refers to the idea that an expansion of private investment raises interest rates and results in a fall in public expenditure.
g If other things remain equal, an increase in government spending on goods and services will lead to an increase in tax revenues and in saving.
h When a tax is progressive, the average rate of tax exceeds the marginal rate.
i A progressive income tax will cause the value of the multiplier to fall as income rises.
j Keynesian analysis indicates that the government should run a Budget deficit in order to eliminate a deflationary gap.

Data response questions

21 *Public Sector Borrowing Requirement* (*£ billion*)

Borrowing requirement of	**1983 forecast**
Central government	11.5
Central government own account	8.5
Local authorities	−0.2
Public corporations	1.1
Unallocated[1]	−1.3
Public sector borrowing requirement	8.2

[1] This item includes sales of public sector assets and an allowance for an expected shortfall in public spending.

The PBSR in 1983–4 is forecast to be just over £8 billion. The high CGBR reflects borrowing for on-lending to local authorities and public corporations. As in 1982–3, they are expected to repay a considerable amount of market debt.

Source: *Financial Statement and Budget Report*, 1983–4, HMSO

a In the light of the extract above, explain the difference between the CGBR (£11.5 billion) and the PSBR (£8.2 billion).
b What are the main ways in which the PSBR is financed?

22 In 1976–7 the net figure for debt interest (on public sector debt) was about £1½ billion. The total net debt interest projected for the present financial year 1982–3 is £6½ billion. Gross debt interest over this period has increased from £6½ billion to £15½ billion. Even the net interest, this year, is expected to be nearly half as much as the projected cost of the defence, health or education programmes. It will cost more than planned spending on housing, law and order, or transport. Gross interest is expected to exceed the cost of all the individual programmes this year, except social security. But it will amount to nearly half the cost of all social security benefits.

It is worth noting that the amount of gross debt interest, for instance, just about doubled between 1976–7 and 1980–1, whereas the total public sector debt in private hands went up by only about a half (in nominal terms) between March 1977 and March 1981.

Source: *Economic Progress Report*, July 1982, HMSO

a The passage mentions one cause of the large increase in interest payments. What was the other main cause?
b What is the difference between *gross interest* and *net interest* on public sector debt?
c What happened to the real burden of interest charges during this period?
d What is the fundamental difference between public expenditure on interest payments and public spending on such items as education, health and transport?

3 The four-sector economy

Exports and imports

This section introduces an international sector into the theory of income determination. The model of the circular flow of income must be modified to include exports (X) and imports (M). Exports are an injection since they represent a demand for domestic output which does not arise within the circular flow of income. Imports are a leakage because they represent expenditure which generates income abroad and not at home. Exports are regarded as autonomous elements in aggregate demand while imports are assumed to be a function of income.

Equilibrium

Some part of planned domestic spending will now comprise a demand for imported goods and services. The demand which determines national income, however, is the demand for *national* output. This means that imports must be deducted from and exports added to total domestic spending. Aggregate demand now comprises $C + I + G + X - M$ and national income will be in equilibrium when $Y = C + I + G + X - M$.

Alternatively, national income will be in equilibrium when

Planned injections = Planned leakages
i.e. when $I + G + X = S + T + M$

The multiplier

The introduction of X and M modifies the formula for the multiplier as follows.

$$\text{The multiplier} = \frac{1}{1 - \text{MPC}} = \frac{1}{\text{MPS} + \text{MRT} + \text{MPM}}$$

where MPM is the marginal propensity to import.

The multiplier process will be set in motion whenever there is a change in one or more of the autonomous components of aggregate demand, or a change in the marginal rate of leakage.

Short answer questions

1 'A planned reduction in imports will clearly reduce the withdrawals from the circular flow of income. The longer-term effect, however, might be a reduction in injections.' Explain.

2 Exports represent part of the national output which leaves the country. How, then, can an increase in exports have an expansionary effect on income?

3 In an economy, direct taxes represent one-quarter of gross income and the propensity to consume is constant at two-thirds of disposable income (there are no transfer payments). Imports represent one-fifth of total consumption. What is the value of the multiplier?

4 When a particular economy is in equilibrium, APC = $0.75Y_d$. Investment is £1250 million, government spending on goods and services is £1500 million and exports are £750 million. The government levies only one tax, an income tax at a constant rate of $0.2Y$. There are no transfer payments, and the average propensity to import is $0.3Y$.

a What is the equilibrium level of income?

b What is the value of the Budget surplus or deficit at the equilibrium level of income?

c What is the value of the balance of payments surplus or deficit at the equilibrium level of income?

5 'The multiplier is a two-edged weapon; it will operate to amplify the effects of any *reduction* in one or more of the autonomous components of aggregate demand.' In the light of this statement consider the following.
In an economy, $T = \frac{1}{10}Y$, $S = \frac{1}{9}Y_d$ and $M = \frac{1}{8}C$. These are no transfer payments. Write down the first three terms of the series which shows how income *falls* when government spending is *reduced* by £500 million.

Multiple choice questions

6 Which of the following would be regarded as a withdrawal from the circular flow of income?

A a rise in public investment
B a surplus on the balance of payments
C a Budget deficit
D a deficit on the balance of payments

7 This question is based on the graph below.

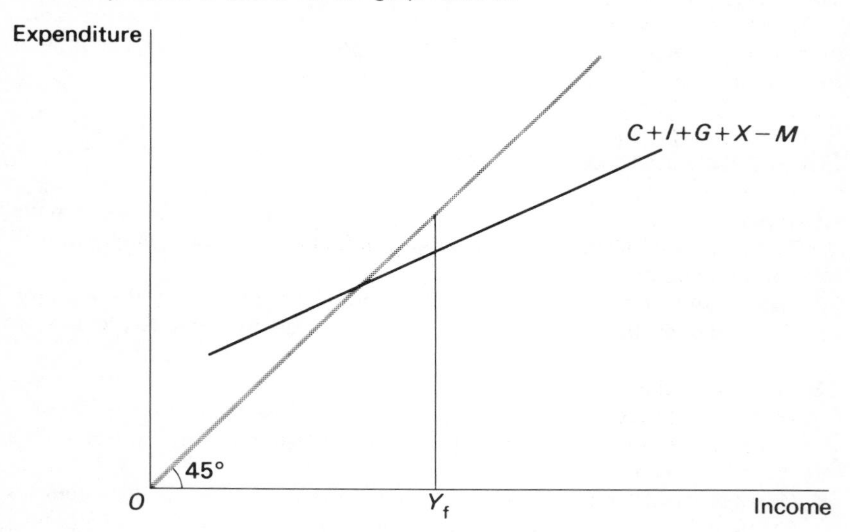

Note: Both axes are drawn to the same scale.

The existing aggregate demand function is $C+I+G+X-M$. OY_f is the full employment level of income. Which of the following measures would tend to remove the deflationary gap?

A an increase in imports
B an increase in the propensity to save
C an increase in an existing Budget surplus
D an increase in exports

8 If an open economy with government is experiencing an inflationary gap, there is likely to be a rise in
1 imports.
2 the rate of interest.
3 unemployment.

A 1, 2, and 3
B 1 and 2 only
C 2 and 3 only
D 1 only
E 3 only

9 If an economy is in equilibrium with unemployed resources, which of the following *cannot* exist?
1 a balance of payments deficit
2 a Budget surplus
3 unplanned investment

A 1, 2, and 3
B 1 and 2 only
C 2 and 3 only
D 1 only
E 3 only

10 Which of the following might cause national income to increase?
1 a reduction in exports
2 a reduction in savings
3 a reduction in imports

A 1, 2, and 3
B 1 and 2 only
C 2 and 3 only
D 1 only
E 3 only

11 Which of the following might be effective in reducing the level of unemployment?
1 an increase in imports
2 an increase in exports
3 a Budget deficit

A 1, 2, and 3
B 1 and 2 only
C 2 and 3 only
D 1 only
E 3 only

12 The national income of an economy is in equilibrium when the following values occur.

$C = 800$ $M = 250$
$T = 300$ $G = 200$
$S = 350$ $X = 300$

The equilibrium level of national income is equal to

A 800
B 1300
C 1450
D 1500
E 2600

True or false?

13 a An increased Budget surplus (given constant government expenditure) will have a deflationary effect on income.
b An increase in the propensity to import will not affect the multiplier.
c If $Y < (C + I + G)$ then $X > M$.
d A fall in autonomous investment expenditure, exports or government spending lowers the level of national income.
e A rise in the rates of taxation, savings or imports raises the level of national income.
f If output increases by 10 per cent then employment must also rise by 10 per cent.
g A given increase in aggregate demand will require a larger Budget deficit if it is to be accomplished by cutting taxes rather than by raising government expenditure.
h It is possible for an economy to be in equilibrium although the balance of payments is in deficit.

Data response questions

14 The table at the top of page 43 gives details of the type and size of the various leakages (or withdrawals) which take place between an increase in GDP and the eventual increase in consumer spending on domestic output. (The figures are hypothetical but may be taken as rough approximations to those which apply to the UK economy.)

Retained profits plus corporation tax	
(as a percentage of increase in GDP)	15%
Personal direct taxation, including NI contributions	
(as a percentage of increase in personal income)	32%
Marginal propensity to consume	
(as a percentage of personal disposable income)	75%
Indirect taxation less subsidies	
(as a percentage of consumer spending)	15%
Import content at factor cost	
(as a percentage of consumer spending)	20%

a Assuming GDP increases by £1000 million, calculate the initial increases in (i) personal disposable income, (ii) consumer spending at market prices and (iii) consumer spending on domestic output at factor cost.
b What is the value of multiplier?

15 This question is based on the diagram below.

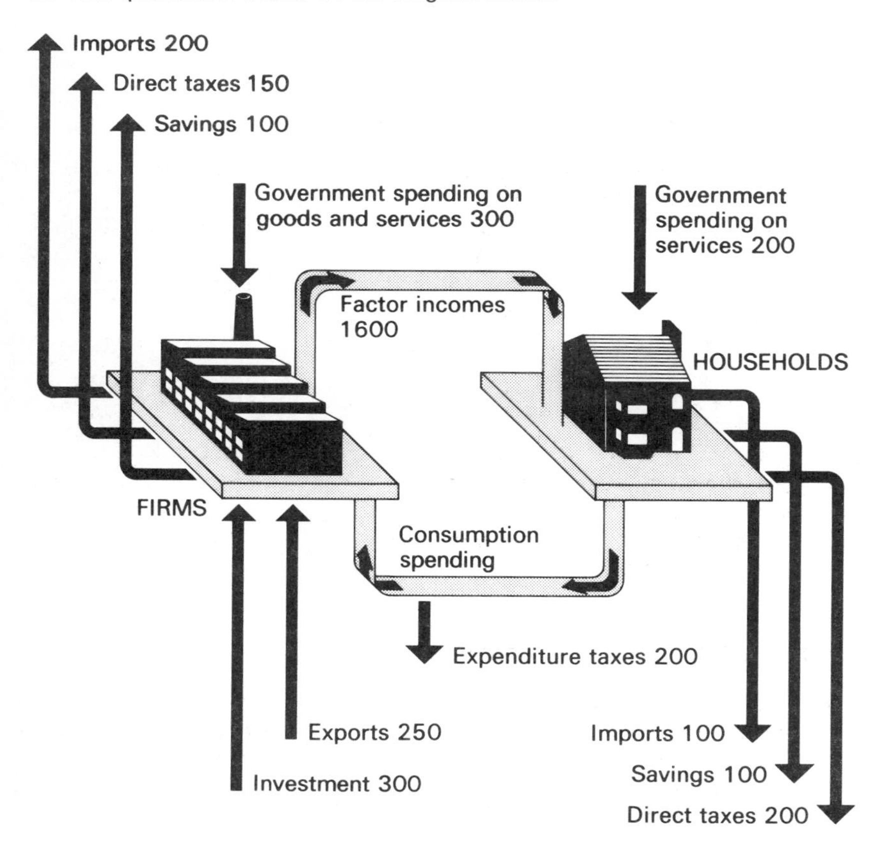

a What is the value of consumption of domestic output at factor cost?
b What is the Gross National Product at factor cost?
c Is this economy in equilibrium? Explain your answer.
d Assuming the rates of withdrawal are constant, what is the value of the multiplier?

Part 4
Money and banking

Money

Money is better defined by its functions than by its form. Anything which serves effectively as a medium of exchange, a store of value, a unit of account and a standard of deferred payments is money. All manner of things have served as money throughout the ages but, nowadays, in most countries, notes, coin and bank deposits are the components of the money supply with bank deposits making up by far the greater part of the money supply in developed countries. The public also holds various extremely liquid assets which, while not functioning as a medium of exchange, serve as a store of value which can easily and quickly be converted into a medium of exchange.

Banks

Banks have many functions but, to an economist, they are particularly important for two reasons.
1 They provide an effective money transmission service (the cheque system).
2 They make loans and advances and, in doing so, they are able to create money in the form of bank deposits. The banks' ability to create deposits is limited because (i) bank deposits are convertible into cash (notes and coin) and (ii) banks can only lend if there is a supply of credit-worthy borrowers.

Banks are profit-seeking institutions and have every incentive to expand their most profitable forms of lending. The need to meet depositors' demands for cash, however, means that they must maintain an adequate supply of liquid assets. The more profitable assets are longer-term loans, but these are not liquid assets, while short-term loans *are* liquid assets but are less profitable than the longer-term ones.

The Bank of England

The Bank of England is the central bank of the UK and has a number of important functions, many of which are connected with the control of the money supply and the banking system. These are the subject of questions in the next section. We can note at this stage that it is the government's bank and the bankers' bank and the transmission of funds between the government and the banking system (via the central bank) has very important effects on both the price and supply of money. The Bank of England is the sole note issuing authority for England and Wales, but this has no relevance for the control of the money supply because notes and coin are supplied to the banking system on request. The central bank plays an important part in the operations of the money market since it acts as a lender of last resort, coming to the aid of the banking system (via the discount houses) when it is short of cash.

The money market

The London money market is a market which deals in short-term and very short-term loans. Several institutions play a part in the operations of this market, including the Bank of England, the commercial banks, branches of overseas banks, acceptance houses and the discount houses. The market deals in a variety of short-term credit instruments such as Treasury bills, local authority bills, commercial bills of exchange, certificates of deposit and government securities with less than one year to run to maturity. The discount houses occupy a key position in the money market because they are the main link between the Bank of England and the rest of the banking system. They enjoy the privilege of borrowing directly from the Bank of England whenever they are short of cash. In absorbing surpluses of short-term funds by borrowing from the banks, the discount houses provide the banks with extremely liquid income-earning assets. At the same time, the fact that these funds are borrowed on such a short-term basis (some are repayable on demand) means that the banks can always make good any shortage of cash by demanding repayment of their loans to the discount houses.

Short answer questions

1 What are the advantages and disadvantages of holding money as an asset?
2 'Successful barter requires a double coincidence of wants.' Explain.
3 What is meant by the terms
a fiduciary issue,
b legal tender,
c token money?
4 Building society deposits are often defined as 'near money'. What particular characteristic of money is lacking in such deposits? What recent developments are bringing about a change in this situation?
5 What is the main component of the UK money supply?
6 'When a bank makes a loan, its assets and liabilities increase by equal amounts.' Explain.
7 If all bank depositors simultaneously exercised their right to convert deposits into cash, the banks would only be able to convert a small percentage of total deposits.
a What is the reason for this state of affairs?
b Does the fact that the banks cannot meet all depositors' demands for cash mean that the banks are insolvent?

8 If all banks maintain a minimum cash ratio of 10 per cent and an individual bank receives a new deposit of £10 000 in cash, to what extent
a will the individual bank be able to create new deposits by making loans?
b will the banking system as a whole be able to create new deposits by making loans?
Assume the public's demand for cash is constant.

9 Banks compete vigorously against each other for funds in the open market and yet lend to one another in the inter-bank market. Why is this so?

10 What is meant by the banks' *clearing arrangements*, and what is their significance in the creation of credit?

11 The following table is a highly simplified hypothetical *combined* balance sheet of the clearing banks.

Liabilities	**£ million**	**Assets**	**£ million**
Deposits	10 000	Cash	2 000
		Securities	3 000
		Loans	5 000
	10 000		10 000

Assume that the banks are *obliged* to maintain a minimum cash ratio of 10 per cent, and that no cash is expected to leak out of the banking system.
a In the UK, what items are included under the heading 'Cash'?
b Why will the banks aim to operate as close as possible to the 10 per cent cash ratio?
c Assume now that the banking system takes action to adjust its balance sheet so that the cash ratio is 10 per cent, but maintains the same proportion between securities and loans. Draw up the balance sheet after the necessary adjustments have been made.

12 Why are *liquidity* and *profitability* described as conflicting objectives in the management of a bank's assets?

13 Identify the main instruments of credit which are bought and sold in the London money market.

14 What is meant by the statement that 'the discount houses agree to cover the tender'?

15 As a lender of last resort the Bank of England will render assistance to the discount houses by discounting *eligible bills* or by lending against the security of such bills. How are eligible bills defined?

16 A security with a nominal value of £5000 and three months to run to maturity is purchased by a discount house for £4800.
a What is the *rate of discount*?
b What *rate of interest* has been charged by the discount house?

17 There are three types of deposit which a commercial bank may hold at the Bank of England:
a cash ratio deposits

b operational deposits
c special deposits
Explain the nature and functions of these different deposits.

18 a In the UK there are several different measures of the money supply. Which measures are defined by the following expressions?

(i) Notes and coin *plus* Private sector sterling sight deposits

(ii) Notes and coin *plus* Private sector sterling sight and time deposits *plus* Public sector sterling deposits

b Explain briefly why different measures of the money supply are used.
c Why would a significant increase in the rate of interest tend to lead to a situation where (ii) is growing faster than (i)?

Multiple choice questions

19 If a commodity is to function effectively as money
1 it must be issued by the state.
2 it must have an intrinsic value.
3 it must be divisible without loss in value.

A 1, 2, and 3
B 1 and 2 only
C 2 and 3 only
D 1 only
E 3 only

20 Other things being equal, total bank deposits are likely to increase if the monetary authorities
1 take action to raise the rate of interest.
2 reduce the size of any liquid assets ratio which banks are obliged to maintain.
3 release their holdings of special deposits.

A 1, 2, and 3
B 1 and 2 only
C 2 and 3 only
D 1 only
E 3 only

21 Which of the following is a liability of a UK commercial bank?
A personal loans
B special deposits at the Bank of England
C bills discounted by the bank

D deposit accounts of customers
E cash ratio deposits at the Bank of England

22 If LA represents the banks' holdings of liquid assets and r the required liquid assets ratio, then following an increase in LA, the maximum possible increase in bank deposits will be equal to

A $\frac{r}{LA}$

B $\frac{\Delta LA}{r}$

C $\frac{r}{\Delta LA}$

D $r \times \Delta LA$

23 A bond with a nominal value of £100 carries a fixed rate of interest of 8 per cent. If the bond matures in one year's time and has a current market value of £96, what is the market rate of interest?

A 12.5%
B 12%
C 8.3%
D 4%

24 The cash ratio deposits which the banks in the UK are obliged to hold at the Bank of England are expressed as a percentage of

A total deposits.
B total assets.
C eligible liabilities.
D liquid assets.

Questions **25**, **26**, and **27** are based on the following items.

A special deposits
B bills of exchange eligible for re-discount at the Bank of England
C money at call
D Treasury bills

25 Which is the commercial banks' most liquid asset?
26 Which is the most illiquid asset?
27 Which item appears on the liabilities' side of the balance sheet of a discount house?

True or false?

28 a In developed countries the cheque is the most important form of money.
b The note issue of the UK is entirely fiduciary.
c Eligible banks are those banks whose acceptances are eligible for re-discount at the Bank of England.
d If a commercial bank buys a security, its assets will rise and its liabilities will fall.
e Every bank loan creates a deposit.
f All the commercial banks' deposits at the Bank of England are counted as part of their cash reserves.
g The discount houses are risk-bearers in the sense that they 'borrow long and lend short'.
h Bank deposits are created when banks acquire assets.
i Current account deposits are the commercial banks' most profitable assets.
j If the note issue is increased there will be a fall in the total value of the securities held by the Issue Department of the Bank of England.

Data response questions

29 The question is based on the following table.

Bank of England weekly return, December 8, 1982 (*£ million*)

Issue Department

Liabilities		Assets	
Notes in circulation	11 271	Government securities	3217
Notes in Banking Department	4	Other securities	8058
	11 275		11 275

Banking Department

Liabilities		Assets	
Public deposits	41	Government securities	456
Special deposits	—	Advances and other accounts	1283
Bankers' deposits	647	Premises and equipment	1011
Reserves and other accounts	2051	Notes and coin	4
Other liabilities	15		
	2754		2754

Source: *Bank of England Quarterly Bulletin*, March 1983

a In view of the enormous scale of government financial transactions, why is the balance in the public deposits account such a small figure?

b What would be the nature and extent of the changes in the above balance sheets if the following transactions were carried out? (Each question refers to the situation shown in the table above.)

(i) The authorities carry out an increase in the note issue by increasing the supply of notes in the Banking Department to £14 million.

(ii) Industrial and commercial companies make tax payments to the Exchequer of £100 million.

(iii) The commercial banks withdraw £2 million in notes from the Banking Department.

(iv) The Bank of England makes a call for £100 million of special deposits.

30 The following extracts were taken from the *Bank of England Quarterly Bulletin* (March 1983):

> Nevertheless, large cash shortages persisted in the money market. These arose from the maturing of earlier assistance to the market and partly from the seasonal strength of the Exchequer finances.
>
> The large cash shortages that persisted throughout the period in the money market meant that the Bank had to buy bills every day.
>
> Late that afternoon rises in clearing banks' base rates to 11% were announced, and the Bank confirmed the new higher level of rates by raising its bill dealing rates, also by 1%.

a (1st extract) Explain in more detail the two reasons given for the persistent large cash shortages in the money market.

b (2nd extract) Explain the mechanism whereby the large cash shortages were removed by the action referred to in this quotation.

c (3rd extract) What is meant by the clearing banks' *base rate*? What does this quotation tell us about the Bank of England's policy, at this particular time, on the market rate of interest?

Part 5

Monetary policy

The main purpose of monetary policy is to regulate the level of aggregate money demand in the economy because the level of demand has an important influence on such things as output, employment, the rate of economic growth, the balance of payments and the rate of inflation. In recent years, monetary policy in the UK has mainly been directed at the control of inflation.

Monetary policy, however, may be used selectively to change the pattern of economic activity (e.g. to stimulate investment and/or to restrict consumption).

The operation of monetary policy is the responsibility of the monetary authorities (i.e. the Treasury and the Bank of England) although the central bank has the task of carrying out the policy.

Monetary policy aims to influence aggregate money demand by acting upon the supply of money. The policy tends to be directed, therefore, at the lending activities of the banks (by acting upon their liquidity) and at the demand for loans (by acting on the rate of interest).

Although the objective of monetary policy is the control of aggregate expenditure, the monetary authorities cannot achieve this objective by direct methods. They can, however, make use of instruments which have some influence on the *determinants* of expenditure. But the effectiveness of these instruments depends upon the prevailing economic conditions. For example, an increase in the rate of interest (an instrument) will not be a very effective deterrent to borrowing (a determinant), if firms are very optimistic about future trading prospects. A restriction on the growth of the money supply may not be an effective restraint on expenditure if it is accompanied by a significant increase in the velocity of circulation of money.

The central bank, therefore, aims to control one or more of the variables (e.g. the liquidity of the banks) which it is believed have an important influence on aggregate expenditure. For the purposes of controlling the growth of the money supply, the Bank of England has at its disposal a variety of instruments (e.g. open market operations).

Short answer questions

1 Generally speaking, it can be said that an asset is more liquid the more swiftly it can be . . . , and the more certain its . . . . Supply the missing words.

2 What is meant by the term liquidity preference?

3 If Y denotes money income (or expenditure) and M denotes the stock of

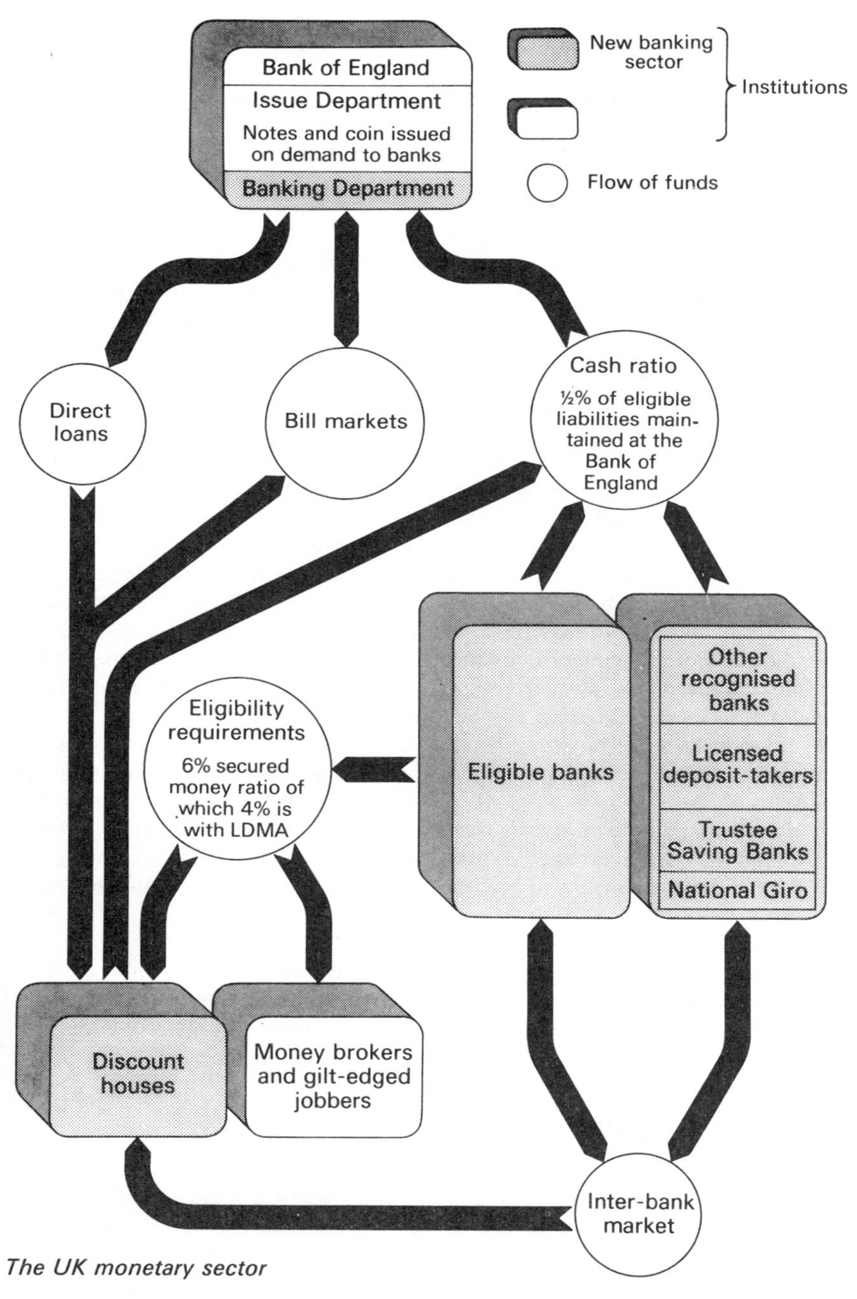

The UK monetary sector

Source: *Barclays Bank Review*, November 1981

money, the relationship between them can be written $Y = aM$. What does a represent?

4 'With a given stock of money, the greater the demand for money to hold, the lower will be the level of income and expenditure.' Explain.

5 'Both Keynesians and monetarists believe that part of the demand for money arises from *transactions* and *precautionary motives*.' Explain the terms in italics.

6 Under what circumstances might it be beneficial to hold money balances (which earn no income) rather than fixed-interest securities?

7 Explain why the rate of interest is inversely related to bond prices.

8 'The stock of money could be an extremely useful target for monetary policy if the link between the stock of money and the level of total expenditure was stable or predictable.' What is the nature of this link?

9 Why is bank lending regarded as a desirable target for monetary policy?

10 How might the use of the rate of interest as an instrument of monetary policy lead to a conflict between the objectives of controlling the money supply and preventing a rise in the exchange rate?

11 Identify one advantage and one disadvantage of using direct controls (i.e. the use of ceilings) on bank lending as an instrument of monetary policy.

12 'With a given target for the money supply, the level of interest rates will tend to be higher, the higher the PSBR.' Explain.

13 Controls on hire-purchase and instalment credit were removed in 1982, but the authorities had made considerable use of these instruments in the 1960s and 1970s. What form did these controls take, and for what particular purpose were they used?

14 'Changes in short-term interest rates engineered by the authorities are one of the main methods of monetary control.' How do the authorities engineer such changes?

15 'Fiscal policy determines the size of the PSBR, but monetary policy determines how it is financed.' Explain.

16 Explain how the sale of securities by the Bank of England to the non-bank public might affect

a the rate of interest.

b the level of private sector bank deposits.

17 The table below illustrates the different stages of a monetary policy aimed at a particular objective with a given operating target. Complete the table by inserting the appropriate information in the first and third columns.

Instruments	**Operating target**	**Intermediate target**	**Objective**
	Liquidity of the banking system		Reducing the rate of inflation by controlling aggregate money demand

Multiple choice questions

18 Other things being equal, an increase in the rate of interest is not likely to

A increase the demand for money.
B cause the exchange rate to appreciate.
C reduce the demand for mortgages.
D lead to a fall in investment.

19 The term *high-powered money* is used to describe

A sight deposits in the commercial banks.
B notes and coin only.
C operational deposits at the central bank only.
D notes and coin and operational deposits at the central bank.

Questions **20**, **21**, **22** and **23** refer to the following components of liquidity.

A notes and coin and private sector sterling sight deposits
B private sector sterling time deposits and public sector deposits
C Treasury bills and bank bills
D deposits with building societies and the National Savings Bank, and National Savings Certificates

Which of the above contains measures of the money supply which

20 are components of £M3 but not M1?
21 are components of PSL1 and PSL2?
22 are found in all the official UK measures of the money supply?
23 are components of PSL2 but not PSL1?

24 Assume that the community as a whole is holding less money than it desires to hold. If other things remain equal, the *community's* attempts to increase money holdings

A will be successful if people are holding bonds which can be exchanged for money.
B will be successful if people are holding physical assets which can be exchanged for money.
C will be unsuccessful and will cause the rate of interest to rise.
D will be unsuccessful and will cause the rate of interest to fall.

25 The stock of money will be an unreliable target for monetary policy if

A the demand for money is related in a predictable way to national income.
B the velocity of circulation is stable.
C people keep a stable proportion of their income in money balances.
D the demand for money is significantly affected by changes in the rate of interest.

26 If the monetary authorities wish to see an expansion of bank lending, they could

1 instruct the government broker to buy securities on the open market.
2 substantially increase the weekly issue of Treasury bills.
3 raise the rate of interest which the Bank of England charges when it provides assistance to the money market.

A 1, 2, and 3
B 1 and 2 only
C 2 and 3 only
D 1 only
E 3 only

True or false?

27 **a** Other things being equal, if there is an increase in the community's liquidity preference, there will also be a reduction in the velocity of circulation.
b A widely held belief that interest rates will rise in the immediate future will cause the speculative demand for money to fall.
c The schedule which relates the supply of money to the rate of interest is described as the liquidity preference schedule.
d If a large number of people move from weekly wage payments to monthly salary payments, the velocity of circulation of money will fall.
e If the demand for money is a stable proportion of the annual value of transactions, the velocity of circulation must also be stable.
f Open market operations enable the central bank to control both the rate of interest and the supply of money.
g The Bank of England uses its position as a monopolist of the note issue (in England and Wales) as a means of controlling the supply of money.
h If rates of interest on call money and overnight loans rise more rapidly than the discount rates on three-month bills, the profitability of the discount houses will be adversely affected.

Data response questions

28 Assume that the central bank purchases £100 million of securities in the open market from private citizens.
a Complete the table below to show the immediate effects on the liabilities and assets of the central bank, the commercial banks and households.

Central Bank

Liabilities	**Assets**
Bankers' deposits	Securities

Commercial Banks

Liabilities	**Assets**
Deposits	Balances at central bank

Households

Liabilities	**Assets**
	Securities
	Bank deposits

b What will be the subsequent effect on the level of bank deposits?
c Make a similar table to show the immediate effects of open market sales of £100 million of securities to private citizens.
d What will be the subsequent effect of these open market sales on the level of bank deposits?

29 The following extract refers to the financing of the PSBR.

> This means that the government has often had to raise interest rates in order to persuade the gilt-edged market that the next move in rates will be down; a technique sometimes known as the Grand Old Duke of York (who marched his men up the hill but then marched them down again).
>
> Source: *The Economist*, 14th January 1981

Explain the nature of the problem that obliges the monetary authorities to take the action referred to in the quotation.

30 The question is based on the following quotation.

> But the fashion for monetary targets does not mean that monetary policy is now single-minded. In practice it still has four aims, which may or may not contradict each other: (1) the containment of inflation, (2) the encouragement of investment and growth, (3) the financing of public sector debt, (4) the containment of pressures on the exchange rate.
>
> Source: *The Economist*, 28th January 1978

a Explain why (1) and (2) may prove to be conflicting aims.
b What is the relationship between (3) and the growth of the money supply?
c Under what circumstances might (2) and (4) be conflicting aims?

31 The question is based on the following quotation.

> The Bank's principal methods of operating in the money market do not have any direct statistical impact on the stock of money, as measured by notes and coin with the public, and bank deposits. For example, when

the Bank buys eligible bills from the market, there is a switch from bills to cash in the assets of the banking system, but no change in deposit liabilities; there is thus only a shift in the statistical counterparts to the money stock, with the Bank taking over, from the rest of the banking system, bill claims on other sectors.[1] Nevertheless, the operations may be designed to influence the stock of money indirectly, through their effect on interest rates. Indeed, the desire to retain a fairly direct influence over interest rates rests on the view that these may have a significant effect on, for example, the demand for money, the demand for credit and the exchange rate, with consequences for the development of the economy more generally.

[1] If the Issue Department buys the bills, there is a corresponding decline in the holding of such bills by the monetary sector. But if the bills are bought by the Banking Department – itself part of the monetary sector – there is merely a shift of holdings within that sector.

Source: *Bank of England Quarterly Bulletin*, March 1982

a Explain (i) how Bank purchases of bills leads to a switch of assets in the banking system and (ii) why deposit liabilities remain unchanged.
b Explain why it is believed that interest rates have a significant effect on (i) the demand for money, (ii) the demand for credit and (iii) the exchange rate.

Part 6

Prices, output and employment

The quantity theory of money

The earliest theory which attempted to link the supply of money with economic activity was the 'crude' quantity theory which assumed that money had one function – to act as a medium of exchange. It also assumed that output was not variable in the short run, so that P (the general price level) varied proportionately with M (the supply of money).

This theory was later refined into an equation of exchange, $MV = PQ$, where V is the income velocity[1] of circulation of money, and Q is the national output. This formulation of the theory, by including V, takes account of the fact that money can serve as a store of value and, by incorporating Q, allows for changes in output. The equation of exchange, however, is a truism: both sides must be equal by definition. It is not a theory because it provides no explanations of the causes of changes in the variables.

During the past thirty-five years or so, the equation has been revived to form the basis of a theory of income determination. Monetarists recognise that V is not constant, but they believe that it is predictable. If this is true, the equation of exchange can be used analytically. PQ may be taken to represent nominal GNP so that the equation may be written as $MV =$ nominal GNP. Thus, the monetarists argue, a careful study of the determinants of M and V will enable the equation to be used to predict the value of GNP.

Demand inflation

The revised quantity theory provides one theory of inflation. If V and Q are reasonably constant, then an increase in M will be associated with an increase in P. According to monetarist theory, money is demanded mainly for transactions purposes so that any increase in the money supply will lead to increased spending on goods and services. Hence, the monetarist theory of inflation is a theory of demand inflation.

The Keynesian theory of inflation is based on the idea of a 'trade-off' between unemployment and inflation. When the economy is operating with a large amount of excess capacity, increases in aggregate demand will increase

[1] The number of times, on average, a unit of money changes hands (per annum) in national income transactions (i.e. in the purchase of final goods and services).

output, reduce unemployment and have little or no effect on the general price level (i.e. trade-off is favourable). If aggregate demand continues to increase when the economy is at or near to full employment, it will be difficult to increase output and the result will be rising prices. The trade-off is unfavourable (i.e. inflation develops) when unemployment is low. In the late 1950s and early 1960s, the Phillips curve was widely accepted as a convincing demonstration of the trade-off between unemployment and inflation.

The conventional Keynesian theory relates inflation to the forces which determine the behaviour of the components of aggregate demand ($C+I+G+X-M$). It is these 'real' forces which determine demand and, it is argued, increases in the money supply do not cause excess demand. The monetary authorities tend to adjust the money supply to finance whatever level of transactions is taking place. Nevertheless inflation can only be sustained if the money supply increases.

Cost inflation

Theories of demand inflation, it seemed, were unable to provide convincing explanations of the type of inflation which developed in the 1970s and early 1980s when many countries experienced high rates of inflation and high rates of unemployment simultaneously. Many economists opted for a cost-push explanation of this period of inflation (or stagflation as it is sometimes described). The cost-push theory explains inflation in terms of increases in the costs of production which are largely independent of the state of demand. According to this theory, prices are not pulled upwards by excess demand, they are pushed upwards by (i) the ability of powerful and militant trade unions to raise wage rates in excess of increases in productivity even when there are surpluses in the markets for labour, (ii) increases in the prices of imported materials (e.g. oil in the 1970s) and (iii) increases in indirect taxation. These factors may initiate a rise in prices but, according to the cost-push theory, the inflationary process is generated and sustained by means of the wage–price spiral.

Unemployment and inflation

The existing theories of inflation did not predict the stagflation of the 1970s and early 1980s. Some economists believe that the trade-off between unemployment and inflation still exists, but structural and institutional changes in the economy have shifted the Phillips curve well to the right. Monetarists assert that there never was a long-run trade-off between inflation and unemployment and that the Phillips curve only illustrates a short-run and unstable relationship. They believe that there is a natural rate of unemployment which is consistent with a stable rate of inflation (which may be zero) and that inflation is caused by governments' attempts to reduce unemployment below this natural rate by increasing aggregate demand. They argue that persistent attempts to maintain unemployment below this natural rate can only result in escalating inflation. According to monetarist theory, the most effective way of reducing the natural rate of unemployment is by removing imperfections in the labour market. Indeed, monetarists would probably classify a significant part of the current UK unemployment as voluntary unemployment in the sense that some labour is unemployed because the level of real wages makes the product of that labour unmarketable.

Governments have been loath to tackle the high levels of unemployment by using the traditional Keynesian reflationary measures since they feared that attempts to increase aggregate demand would only increase the rate of inflation. Many economists believe that the monetarist remedy for inflation (a severe restriction on the growth of the money supply) would succeed only at the cost of intolerably high levels of unemployment. They argue, therefore, that the cost pressures which sustain inflation can only be removed by means of an effective incomes policy.

Short answer questions

1 In a certain economy over a period of five years, the money supply increased in the ratio 100:110, while real national income increased in the ratio 100:112. If the velocity of circulation of money remained constant, what happened to prices over this period of time? Explain your answer.

2 Distinguish between the *transactions* velocity of money and the *income* velocity of money.

3 Microeconomic theory indicates that excess demand will be eliminated by a rise in prices. Why then, in the case of demand inflation, does a rise in the general price level not choke off excess demand?

4 Indicate two different ways in which excess aggregate demand may arise under conditions of full employment.

5 Two schools of thought, generally described as Keynesian and monetarist, tend to differ on the economic effects of changes in the rate of interest.

	Keynesian theory	**Monetarist theory**
The demand for money	Very responsive to changes in the rate of interest	Not very responsive to changes in the rate of interest
Expenditure on goods and services	Not very responsive to changes in the rate of interest	Very responsive to changes in the rate of interest

On the basis of these highly simplified distinctions, explain briefly the sequence of events which would follow an increase in the supply of money

a according to Keynesian theory, and

b according to monetarist theory.

6 Assume that

(i) a once-and-for-all increase in the prices of imported materials raises the UK general price level by 10 per cent,

(ii) wages comprise 70 per cent of total costs, there is no increase in productivity and cost increases are fully passed on as price increases and

(iii) trade unions always press for and succeed in obtaining wage increases which fully compensate for price increases.

Show that if other elements of costs do not increase, the inflationary process will gradually peter out.

7 Why is the 'comparability argument' as a basis of wage claims often cited as an important factor in cost-push inflation?

8 If prices are rising and the central bank wishes to hold interest rates at a steady level, what will happen to the supply of money? Explain your answer.

9 This question is based on the graph below.

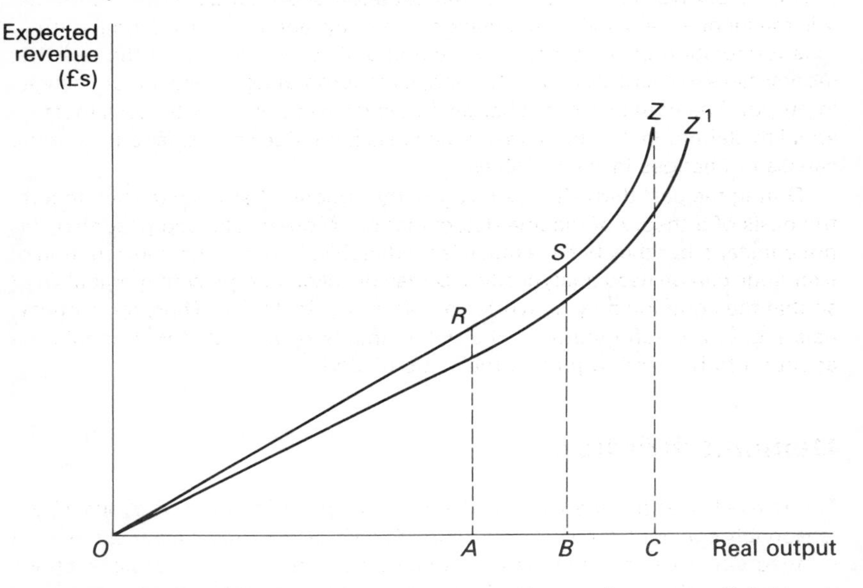

In the graph, *OZ* represents an aggregate supply curve. Points on this curve show the different amounts of total expenditure which would be just sufficient to persuade firms to supply the corresponding outputs.

a When the existing supply curve is *OZ*,

(i) what is the supply price at output *OA*?

(ii) what is the supply price at output *OB*?

(iii) why is the supply curve a straight line for outputs up to *OA*?

(iv) why does the supply curve terminate at output *OC*?

b What might cause the aggregate supply curve to move from *OZ* to OZ^1?

10 This question is based on the graph below.

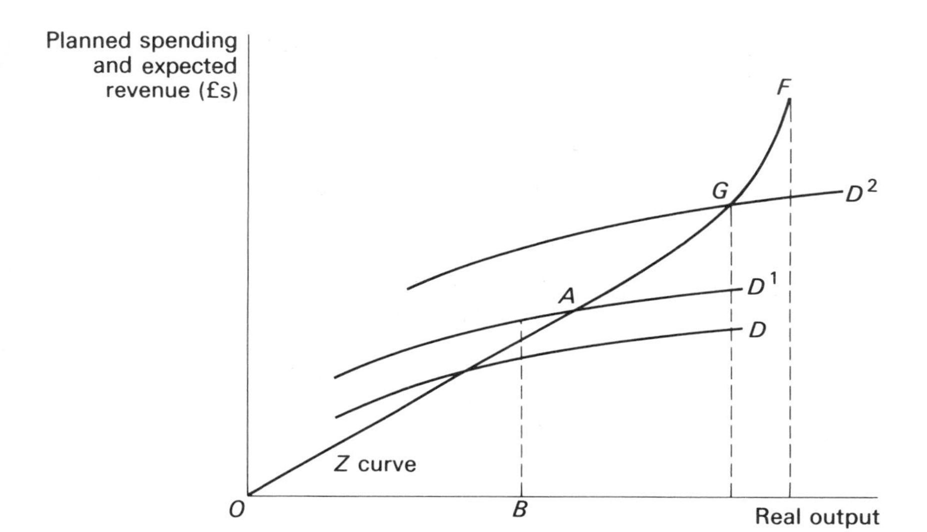

The graph above combines aggregate money demand curves (D, D^1, D^2) with the aggregate supply curve (Z). These demand curves show planned money expenditures on goods and services at different levels of real output.

a What factors might cause the demand curve to move upwards, for example from D to D^1 or from D^1 to D^2?

b What would happen to the general price level if demand increased from D to D^1?

c Assume that the existing demand curve is D^1 and national output is at the level OB.

(i) Why is this an unstable level of national income?

(ii) In what way will income change, and what forces will cause it to change?

d If the curve D^2 represents the present state of demand, what will be the extent of the increase in the general price level if demand is increased so as to achieve full-employment output?

11 The inflationary process will be a converging one (i.e. the rate of inflation will gradually diminish) if aggregate money demand increases at a slower rate than total factor income. Give two reasons why this may be a possibility.

12 Why are 'expectations' included as an important factor in many modern theories of inflation?

13 'Cost-push inflation cannot continue unless the price and wage increases are validated by the government.' Explain.

14 In the diagram below, aggregate demand and supply curves are used to show the effects of an increase in the domestic costs of production. Develop the diagram to illustrate how a cost-push process of inflation may be generated.

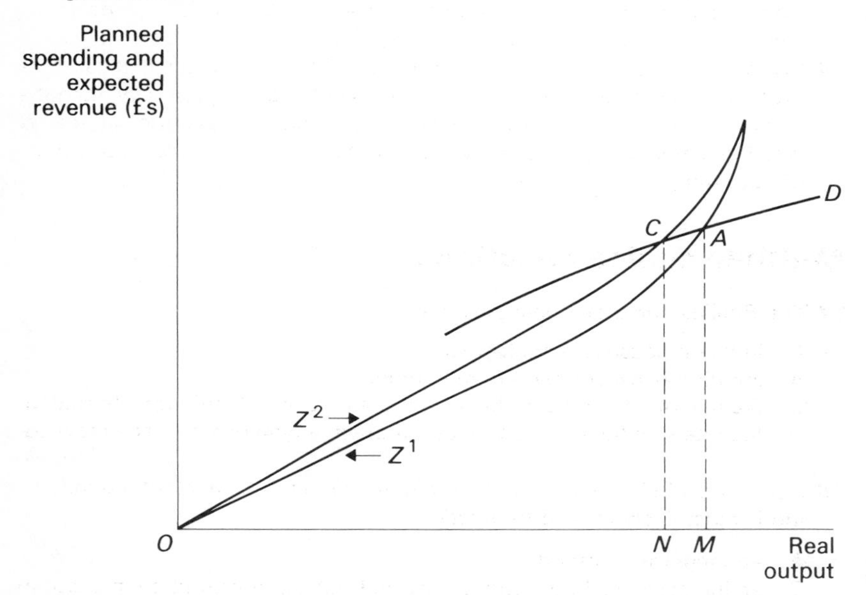

15

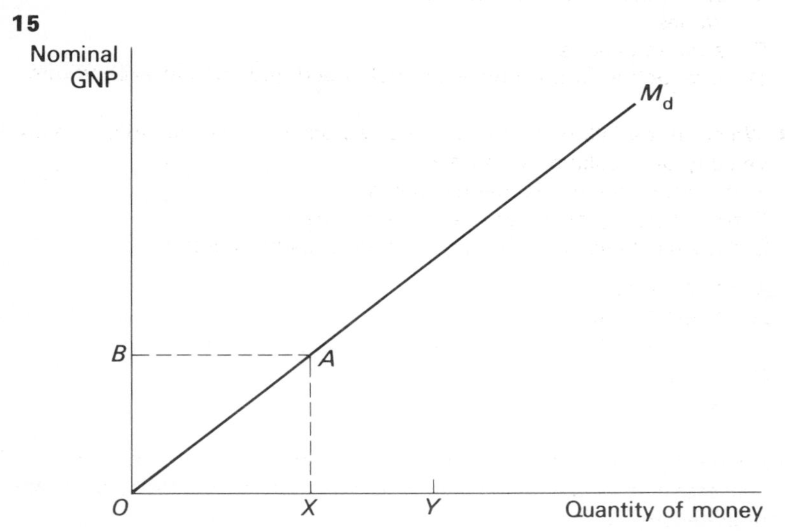

The graph above assumes a stable relationship between the demand for money (M_d) and nominal GNP.

a What does the fact that M_d is a straight line tell us about the velocity of circulation?

b Suppose initially that the stock of money was *OX* and nominal GNP was *OB*, so that the demand for money was exactly equal to the supply of money. Now suppose that the stock of money increases to *OY*. Explain the developments which will bring about a new equilibrium.

16 Monetarist theory states that if the output of goods and services takes its own course according to the productive potential of the economy, then the rate at which prices will rise depends in a predictable way on the rate at which the money supply is allowed to rise. What is the *fundamental* underlying assumption in this theory?

Multiple choice questions

17 The Phillips curve demonstrates that

A inflation causes unemployment.
B inflation is caused by the trade unions.
C the rate of inflation and the rate of unemployment are inversely related.
D the rate of inflation and the rate of unemployment are directly related.

18 Assuming a full-employment level of national output, which of the following is most likely to lead to inflation?

A an increase in imports
B an increase in labour productivity without a corresponding increase in wages
C a fall in exports
D a reduction in taxation with unchanged government expenditure

19 Which of the following 'institutional factors' has/have an influence on the velocity of circulation of money?

1 the frequency of income payments
2 the efficiency of the payments mechanism
3 the availability of highly-liquid income-earning assets

A 1, 2, and 3
B 1 and 2 only
C 2 and 3 only
D 1 only
E 3 only

20 According to monetarist ideas, which of the following is/are likely to be successful in achieving a permanent reduction in the natural rate of unemployment?

1 a cut in direct and indirect taxation
2 an increase in the money supply

3 increased government spending on retraining schemes for labour

A 1, 2, and 3
B 1 and 2 only
C 2 and 3 only
D 1 only
E 3 only

21 The question is based on the following information.

Year	**1**	**2**	**3**
Retail sales (volume)	100	105	115
Retail sales (value)	100	110	130

On the basis of this information it can be said that
1 the standard of living has risen.
2 unemployment has fallen.
3 the cost of living has risen.

A 1, 2, and 3
B 1 and 2 only
C 2 and 3 only
D 1 only
E 3 only

22 The following information refers to a country where consumers purchase only three commodities.

	Index of prices Year 1	**Index of prices Year 2**	**Consumers' expenditure Year 1 (£ million)**
Commodity A	100	150	100
Commodity B	100	90	300
Commodity C	100	120	200

Between years 1 and 2, the general level of prices rose by

A 20%
B 16.6%
C 11%
D 10%

23 The following are possible causes of inflation. Which of them is the most likely cause of cost inflation?

A an expansion of bank lending
B a budget deficit
C a rise in world commodity prices
D a fall in the rate of investment

24 The equation of exchange, $MV = PT$, is true

A only if firms have excess capacity.
B only if V is constant.
C only if the economy is fully employed.
D by definition.

True or false?

25 a A fall in the value of money means a fall in the standard of living.
b Changes in the prices of some commodities have a much greater effect on the measured rate of inflation than similar changes in the prices of other commodities.
c Other things being equal, an increase in the volume of imports will tend to increase the rate of inflation.
d Unemployment is positively related to the rate of inflation because increasing unemployment means a falling supply of goods and services.
e The quantity theory of money predicts that a change in the money supply leads to a proportionate change in real output.
f The natural rate of unemployment is defined as an irreducible minimum level of unemployment.
g Wage-push inflation occurs when real wages rise faster than money wages.
h In inflationary conditions borrowers tend to be 'gainers' and lenders tend to be 'losers'.
i Monetarists argue that all inflation is demand inflation.

Data response questions

26 The graph on page 68 shows a short-run Phillips curve (P_2) as used in monetarist explanations of the relationships between unemployment and inflation. Assume that, initially, the economy is at point A, with a stable rate of inflation of 2 per cent per annum and that inflation is expected to remain at 2 per cent. Unemployment is at its natural rate of 5 per cent. The Phillips curve P_2 shows the relationship between unemployment and inflation when inflation is expected to remain at 2 per cent.

Now assume that the government wishes to reduce unemployment to 3 per cent and proceeds to increase aggregate money demand. Explain the subsequent developments as predicted by monetarist theory.

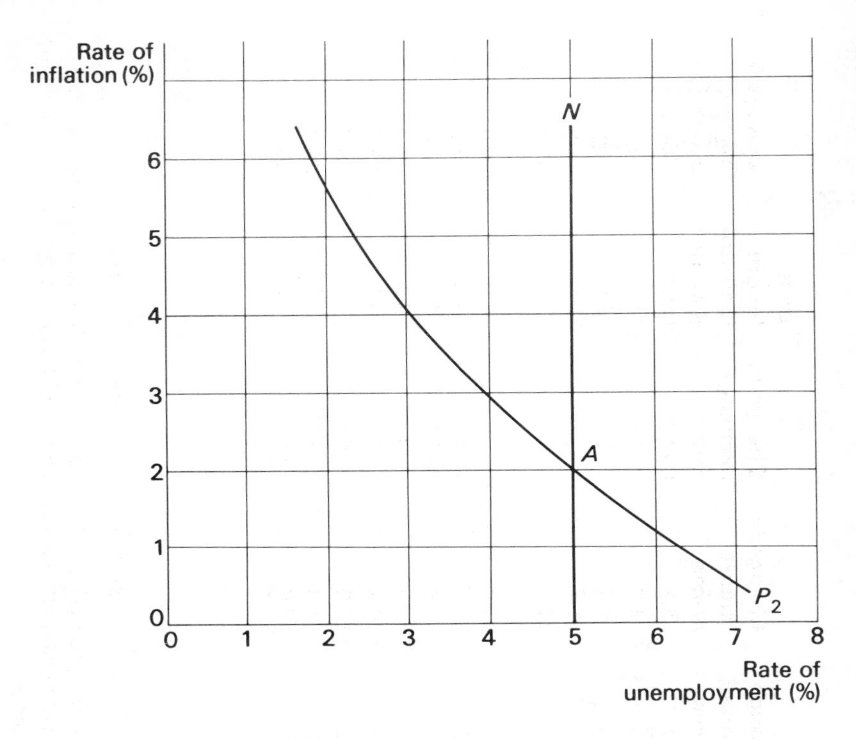

Graph for question **26**

27 The question is based on the following quotation.

> One of the more remarkable features of the Phillips curve and one which distinguishes it from most similar studies, was that it was found to be highly reliable in predicting increases in wages during much later periods of time than the years 1861–1913 which had been used to derive the equation. Thus Phillips was able to show a very close correspondence for 1948–57 between the wage changes implied by his relationship and those which actually took place. The Phillips curve was also very accurate in predicting wage increases over the period 1958–66 which was after the study had been published.
>
> After the mid-1960s, however, the pure Phillips curve became increasingly unreliable as a guide to the rate of wage inflation.

Source: Prest and Coppock, *The UK Economy*, 9th edition, Weidenfeld and Nicolson

What factors might explain the breakdown of the relationship portrayed by the Phillips curve?

28 *Possible contributors to UK inflation, 1970–82*

Year	Unemployment percentage[1]	Unfilled vacancies[2] (%)	Change in wage rates[3] (%)	Change in retail prices (%)	Change in import prices (%)	Change in exchange rate[4] (%)	Days lost in industrial disputes (m.)	Change in money stock[5] (%)
1970	2.5	0.8	9.9	6.4	4.5	−1.0	11.0	9.5
1971	3.3	0.6	12.9	9.4	4.7	−0.2	13.6	13.9
1972	3.6	0.6	13.8	7.1	5.7	−3.6	23.9	24.5
1973	2.6	1.4	13.7	9.2	27.9	−9.3	7.2	26.3
1974	2.5	1.3	19.8	16.1	46.2	−3.1	14.8	10.2
1975	3.9	0.6	29.5	24.2	14.0	−7.7	6.0	6.6
1976	5.2	0.6	19.3	16.5	22.2	−14.3	3.3	9.5
1977	5.7	0.7	6.6	15.8	15.6	−5.3	10.1	10.0
1978	5.6	0.9	14.1	8.3	3.9	3.7	9.4	15.0
1979	5.3	1.0	15.0	13.4	10.1	7.1	29.5	12.7
1980	6.7	0.6	18.0	18.0	15.0	10.1	12.0	18.6
1981	10.4	0.4	10.0	11.9	9.3	−1.2	4.2	24.4
1982	12.0	0.4	6.7	8.6	7.0	−4.8	7.9	20.4

[1] Excluding school leavers
[2] Adult vacancies
[3] Weekly rates for manual workers
[4] Effective exchange rate
[5] £M3 change during year

Sources: Prest and Coppock, *The UK Economy*, 9th edition, Weidenfeld and Nicolson, and *Economic Trends*, HMSO March 1983

The table above groups together the main factors that have been suggested as causes of or contributors to the rate of inflation. What light do these statistics throw on the possible causes of inflation during the period 1970–82? Indicate ways in which the various causes or contributors might be linked to one another.

Part 7

The balance of payments and the rate of exchange

The balance of payments

The balance of payments is an account which records financial transactions between the residents of one country (i.e. firms, households and public authorities) and residents of other countries.

Foreign currency payments and receipts arise from a wide variety of transactions, which are grouped into sections in the balance of payments.

1 The current account records the payments and receipts arising from visible trade (the exports and imports of goods) and invisible trade (exports and imports of services, property income and transfers).

2 The capital account records the long-term and short-term capital flows into and out of the country.

3 Official financing Like all balance sheets, the balance of payments must balance in the accounting sense of the term. Thus, if there is a deficit on the current plus capital accounts, the final section of the balance of payments (i.e. official financing) must show how the deficit has been financed. Likewise, this section will show how a surplus has been allocated. Transactions in this account are described as accommodating items and include changes in the official foreign currency reserves and loans from (or repayments to) international institutions, including the IMF.

The rate of exchange

The rate of exchange is the external value of a currency expressed in terms of gold or a major currency, such as the dollar, or as a weighted average of its values in terms of several major currencies. The rate of exchange may be determined in a number of ways.

1 A fixed exchange rate The government may choose to express the value of the currency in one of the ways described above and then declare that it will hold the exchange rate at this fixed parity. More usually, it undertakes to hold the external value of the currency within some narrow limits on each side of the declared parity. This means that the central bank will have to intervene in the foreign exchange market as a buyer or seller whenever market forces tend to move the exchange rate outside the permitted band of fluctuation. When it is clear that the currency is seriously overvalued or undervalued at the fixed parity, it will be necessary to devalue or revalue the currency.

2 Floating exchange rates Under this system there is no official intervention in the foreign exchange market and the external value of the currency is determined by the unrestricted operation of the forces of supply and demand.
3 Managed exchange rates This means that no official parities are declared or maintained, but the monetary authorities intervene to keep the exchange rate higher or lower than it would be in a free market. This type of intervention is often described as 'dirty floating'. Intervention, however, may be purely for the purpose of 'smoothing' (i.e. to prevent sudden and sharp changes in the exchange rate).

Balance of payments equilibrium

A balance of payments equilibrium means that over a period of years the flows into and out of the country from current and capital account transactions are equal. In other words, over this time period, the accommodating items sum to zero. It must be borne in mind, however, that such an equilibrium may be obtained at relatively high cost in terms of unemployment, restrictions on economic growth and infringements of international obligations (e.g. the use of tariffs and quotas).

A persistent deficit in the balance of payments may be dealt with in a number of ways. If the exchange rate is fixed, the government will use deflationary measures, import controls or devaluation or some combination of these measures. If the exchange rate is floating, the market mechanism may eliminate the deficit. In theory, at least, the currency will depreciate and alter the relative prices of exports and imports to an extent which is sufficient to bring about an equilibrium. Recent experience has shown, however, that if the exchange rate is allowed to rise and fall freely, there may be unacceptable effects on the domestic economy; hence the widespread use of managed exchange rates.

A persistent surplus on the balance of payments is often regarded as an indicator of successful economic management rather than a problem. But one country's surplus is another country's deficit, and countries suffering from persistent deficits might be forced to erect barriers to trade. This could lead to a growth of protectionism and a decline in world trade. Revaluation, the removal of import restrictions and an expansion of aggregate demand are obvious measures for the removal of a persistent trade surplus.

Short answer questions

1 If $Y > (C + I + G)$, will there be a surplus or a deficit on the balance of payments? Explain your answer.
2 Why does a withdrawal of foreign currency from the official reserves appear in the official financing section of the balance of payments as a positive item?

3 Why are some items in the balance of payments described as accommodating items?

4 What does the 'balancing item' balance?

5 In which sections of the balance of payments would the following items appear?

a the earnings of a British symphony orchestra from a tour in the USA
b the winnings of a UK citizen in an overseas lottery
c the repayment of a loan to the IMF
d the purchase by a Japanese company of a factory in the UK

6 The question refers to the balance of payments items in the following table. (The figures are hypothetical.)

	£ million
Exports	8500
Long-term investment overseas (net)	−250
Balancing item	+200
Imports	−9000
Interest, profits and dividends	+700
Changes in foreign currency reserves	(i)
Other invisibles	+500
Repayment of loan to IMF	800
Balance for official financing	(ii)
Government transactions in services	+450

a What is the invisible balance?
b What is the current balance?
c Give the appropriate figures and signs for items (i) and (ii).
d Which item gives the overall balance of payments position?

7 What is meant by the term 'non-market balance' when it is applied to the balance of payments?

8 Why has the large-scale participation of foreign companies in the development of the North Sea oilfields tended to reduce the surplus on the invisible account of the UK balance of payments?

9 Distinguish between a *depreciation* of the external value of a currency and *devaluation* of a currency.

10 If the pound sterling were to be devalued by 10 per cent in terms of the dollar, by what percentage would the sterling price of American imports increase? Explain your answer.

11 When the external value of a currency falls, the subsequent effect on the balance of payments is sometimes described as the *J curve effect*. What does this mean?

12 In a free market the following official rates of exchange were quoted on a particular day: £1 = $2.0, £1 = 5.0 fr.

a What is the equilibrium rate of exchange between dollars and francs?
b If trading began to take place at a rate of $1.0 = 2.25 fr., what type of speculative activity would be encouraged?

c Assuming no transactions cost, show how a speculator with 4500 fr. could take advantage of the exchange rate $1.0 = 2.25 fr. to increase his or her holdings of francs.

13 'As far as exports are concerned, devaluation will have a favourable price effect, but it may also have an unfavourable income effect.' Explain.

14 'The dollar is the major reserve currency.'
a What is meant by a *reserve currency*?
b How can the supply of dollars as a reserve currency be increased?

15 **a** What are Special Drawing Rights?
b What is their importance in international liquidity?

16 In what way does the existence of a *forward market* diminish the uncertainty associated with floating exchange rates?

17 'When a country is on a fixed exchange rate, *internal* policy objectives might have to be sacrificed to the *external* policy objectives of protecting the balance of payments and supporting the exchange rate.' Explain.

18 Why is the holding of a reserve fund of convertible foreign currencies, gold and SDRs important to a country on a fixed exchange rate but of less importance to a country operating a *freely* floating exchange rate?

19 What circumstances might lead to a large increase in the flow of 'hot money' into a country?

20 How are exchange rates determined according to the Purchasing Power Parity Theory?

Multiple choice questions

21 If the demand for imports is price inelastic (i.e. $0 < E_d < 1$), then a depreciation in the external value of a currency will
1 increase the volume of imports.
2 cause more foreign currency to be spent on imports.
3 cause more domestic currency to be spent on imports.

A 1, 2, and 3
B 1 and 2 only
C 2 and 3 only
D 1 only
E 3 only

22 This question refers to the official financing section of the UK balance of payments.

	£ million
Account with the IMF	+1000
Changes in the official reserves	−500
Accounts with foreign central banks	−300

Which of the following statements is/are correct?
1 The UK repaid foreign currency to the value of £1000m. to the IMF.
2 Foreign currency to the value of £500m. was withdrawn from the reserves.
3 Foreign currency to the value of £300m. was repaid to foreign central banks.

A 1, 2, and 3
B 1 and 2 only
C 2 and 3 only
D 1 only
E 3 only

23 The *immediate* effect(s) of a depreciation of sterling would be
1 an improvement in the UK terms of trade.
2 that UK imports became dearer in terms of foreign currency.
3 that UK exports became cheaper in foreign markets.

A 1, 2, and 3
B 1 and 2 only
C 2 and 3 only
D 1 only
E 3 only

24 Which of the following policies, if used as a means of improving the balance on current account, might be described as expenditure-switching measures?
1 subsidies to home producers
2 devaluation
3 tariffs

A 1, 2, and 3
B 1 and 2 only
C 2 and 3 only
D 1 only
E 3 only

25 Long-term investment by UK firms in overseas countries will have
1 an immediate adverse effect on the capital account of the balance of payments.
2 a longer-term favourable effect on the current account of the balance of payments.
3 an immediate adverse effect on the sterling balances in the Exchange Equalisation Account.

A 1, 2, and 3

B 1 and 2 only
C 2 and 3 only
D 1 only
E 3 only

26 Which of the following conditions would be most favourable to a country carrying out a devaluation as a means of improving its balance of payments?

A A high proportion of its imports consists of foodstuffs and raw materials.
B Its exports have to compete with many close substitutes in foreign markets.
C The demand for its exports is price inelastic.
D The elasticity of supply of its exports is relatively low.

Questions **27**, **28** and **29** are based on the diagram below, which shows the supply and demand conditions for pounds in the foreign exchange market. Starting in each case from an initial equilibrium position of *Z*, you are asked to say what the equilibrium rate of exchange would be after the change described.

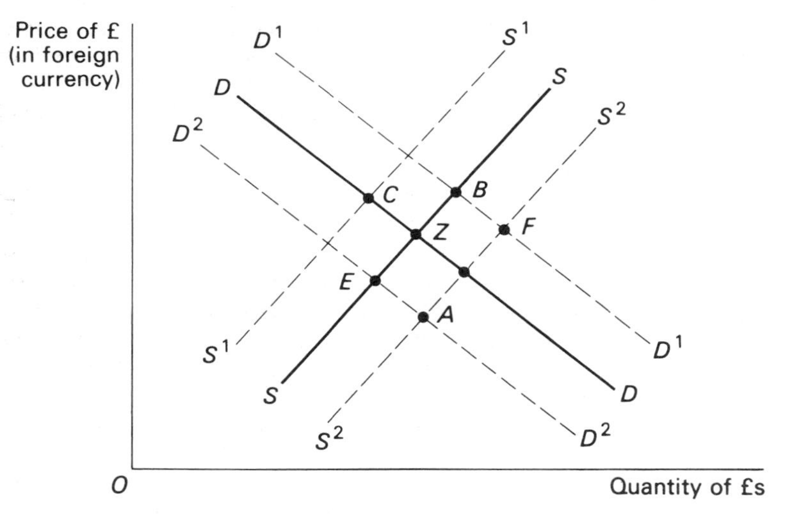

27 A reduction in the number of UK citizens taking holidays abroad.
28 Increased investment by foreign firms in the domestic economy.
29 A reduction in the demand for the UK's exports *and* an increase in its imports.

30 Assume that exchange rates are being allowed to float. Over a period of one year the external value of the currency of country X (the groat) fell from 20 groats = £1 to 15 groats = £1. Which of the following would have been the most likely cause of the depreciation of the groat?

A There was a significant increase in exports from country X.
B Country X imposed a variety of import controls.
C The inflation rate in country X had been much higher than the rates in other countries.
D Country X had been pursuing a deflationary policy.

True or false?

31 **a** The IMF imposes no conditions when a country borrows from its reserve tranche.
b After a long period in deficit, the contribution of North Sea oil moved the UK balance of trade into surplus in the late 1970s.
c If a country devalues its currency, the costs of servicing its overseas debt will increase.
d Gold is still an important component of international liquidity.
e A major part of total world liquidity consists of inconvertible foreign currencies.
f A positive balancing item reflects an unrecorded net outflow of foreign currency.
g A feature of the Eurocurrency market is the fact that people can borrow currency A in financial centre B for use in country C.
h The servicing of substantial foreign debts adds heavily to the outflows in the current account of the balance of payments.
i A British company acquiring a factory in a foreign country is an example of portfolio investment.
j When a country operating a fixed rate of exchange is experiencing a relatively high rate of inflation, its currency will tend to be overvalued in the foreign exchange market.
k The World Bank makes loans for balance of payments financing while the IMF makes loans for development projects.
l Strictly speaking, member countries purchase rather than borrow foreign currencies from the IMF.

Data response questions

32 This question is based on the following quotation.

A weaker pound is music to exporters' ears
Three imponderables put the full effect on output in doubt:
1 Exporters' profit margins Some businesses may exploit the pound's depreciation by widening profit margins rather than allowing prices to fall to stimulate orders. Firms' balance sheets would be eased, but output would be boosted only if bigger profits drew more firms on to the export trail.
2 World trade A devaluation will have a strong effect on British

output only if foreign demand is sufficiently strong to increase purchases of British goods. This year, world trade may have actually shrunk for the first time in 30 years: even the optimists only forecast 3–4% growth next year. According to the London stockbrokers, Simon and Coates, British exports respond only feebly to rises in world trade – by 0.7% for every 1% rise in trade – whereas British imports rise by 1.6% for every 1% rise in GDP.

3 Inflation By raising import prices, a cheaper pound is bound to slow inflation's fall. By how much depends on whether the dollar falls; whether importers, too, adjust their profit margins rather than their prices; and on whether expectations of future inflation feed into wage demands.'

Source: *The Economist*, 27th November 1982

a Why is a weaker pound welcomed by exporters?

b Explain how depreciation allows exporters to choose between higher profit margins and expanded sales at lower prices.

c Which information in section **2** points to a real problem in using aggregate demand as a means of reducing unemployment?

d Why should a cheaper pound 'slow inflation's fall'? Why is the extent of the fall in the value of the dollar relevant to this problem?

e Explain the reference in section **3** to the adjustment of importers' profit margins.

33 The table below provides information on the conditions in the foreign exchange market during a particular time period. (The figures are hypothetical.)

Rate of exchange	Number of dollars offered for pounds (millions)	Number of pounds offered for dollars (millions)
£1 = $2.4	1200	3500
£1 = $2.2	2200	3000
£1 = $2.0	3000	2500
£1 = $1.8	3600	2000
£1 = $1.6	4000	1500
£1 = $1.4	4200	1000
£1 = $1.2	4200	500

a Use the information provided to construct a graph showing the demand for and supply of pounds in relation to the dollar.

b What is the equilibrium rate of exchange?

c If the UK monetary authorities were committed to maintain a rate of exchange of £1 = $2.0, what would be the nature and extent of their intervention in the market?

d What particular fund would be utilised when the authorities intervene in the market?

Part 8

Economic growth

Economic growth is a major objective of government economic policy because it is the key to a higher material standard of living. Growth refers to an increase in the capacity to produce; that is, the achievement of a greater volume of output per unit of input. Growth, therefore, need not take the form of an increase in real GNP; it can take the form of a constant output with a reduced input. In other words, the benefits of economic growth may be taken in the form of increased leisure. In growing economies, most people have chosen a combination of more leisure and more income.

Although it is possible to identify some of the main determinants of economic growth, the reasons for the discrepancies between the rates of growth achieved by different countries are imperfectly understood. Countries undertaking the same rates of net investment, for example, often display very different rates of growth.

A faster rate of economic growth imposes various costs on the community, the most obvious one being the forgone alternative of higher levels of current consumption as more resources are devoted to capital creation. There are, however, other costs of a social nature which have attracted more and more attention in recent years. There seems little doubt, however, that the great majority of people regard economic growth as a desirable objective. The *potential* for economic growth has been clearly demonstrated during the post-war period. Between 1950 and 1976, gross world product per head increased by 225 per cent. The increase in total output was significantly greater than this because world population itself was also growing rapidly.

The cumulative nature of economic growth means that it is very difficult for developing nations to 'catch up' with the developed countries. If a developed country and a developing country grow at the same rate, the absolute gap between them widens. The following quotation demonstrates the magnitude of the gap in living standards between the rich and poor countries (many of whom have relatively high population growth rates).

> Assuming more reasonably that all these groups (i.e. low income countries, middle income countries and industrialised countries) grow at their 1970–6 average rates, it will be AD 2220 before middle income countries match the industrialised ones; the low income countries would slip farther and farther behind.
>
> Source: *The Economist*, 3rd February 1979

Short answer questions

1 Which of the following concepts provides the best indicator of changes in living standards?
a changes in total output
b changes in output per man-hour
c changes in output per capita

2 Why, as an economy grows, does *real income per person* tend to grow more slowly than *the economy's productive capacity per person*?

3 This question is based on the diagram below.

Production possibility curves

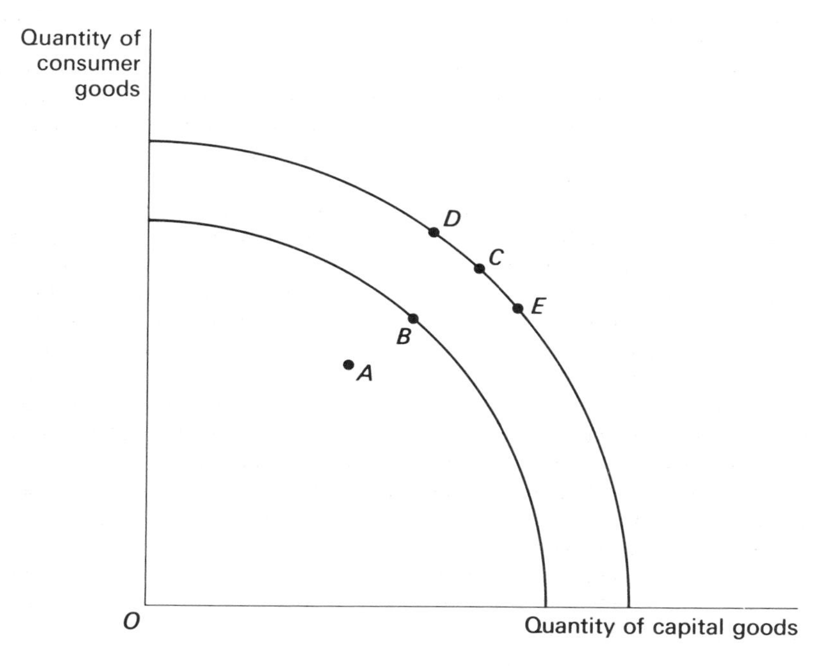

a Distinguish between a movement from *A* to *B* and a movement from *B* to *C*.
b If the economy were at point *C*, which of the following movements would lead to an increase in the productive capacity of the economy?
(i) *C* to *E*
(ii) *C* to *D*
Explain your answer.

4 Why does economic growth make it easier for a government to carry out a policy designed to reduce the degree of inequality in the distribution of income?

5 It has been said that the low growth rates in some developing countries are due to the fact that these countries are caught up in the *vicious circle of poverty*. What is the meaning of the term in italics?

6 

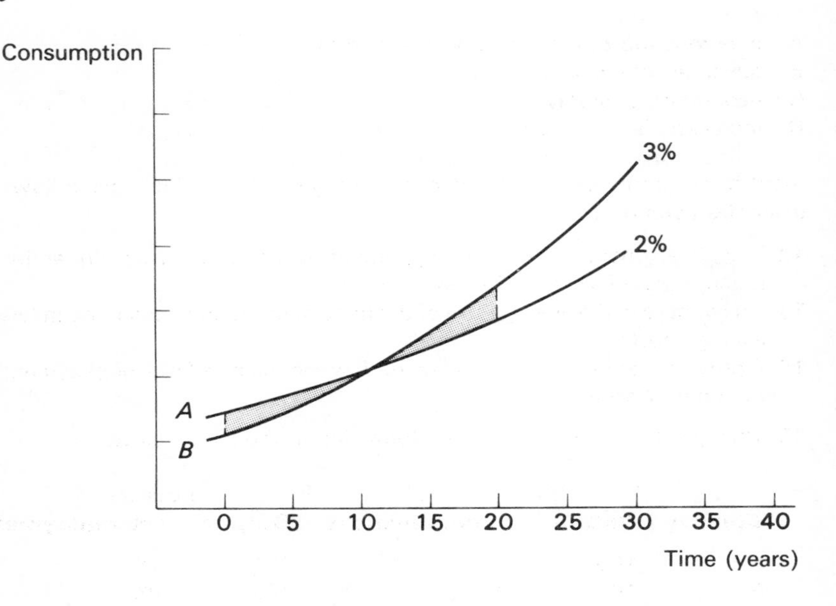

In the diagram above, the two lines *A* and *B* show the rate of increase of consumption when the economy is growing at 2% per annum and 3% per annum respectively. Assume that the economy has been growing at 2% per annum and a reallocation of resources is undertaken in year 0 in order to increase the growth rate to 3% per annum. Use this diagram to explain the *opportunity costs* of growth.

7 a If Y represents actual income and Y_f represents potential income, what does the expression $\frac{Y}{Y_f} \times 100$ represent?

b under what circumstances would a significant increase in $\frac{Y}{Y_f} \times 100$ be possible?

8 'If the average and marginal efficiencies of capital are declining, the capital/output ratio will be increasing.' Explain.

9 How may a greater output per unit of input be achieved in the absence of technical progress or any change in the quality of the factors of production?

10 'In a growing economy, the critical amount of investment is not that which is needed to close a deflationary gap.' What, then, is the critical amount of investment?

11 How does technical progress affect the marginal efficiency of capital?

Multiple choice questions

Questions **12**, **13**, and **14** are based on the following sources of economic growth.

A a more favourable allocation of resources
B advances of knowledge
C economies of scale
D increased factor inputs

Identify the particular source of economic growth to which the following examples belong.

12 The replacement of worn-out equipment by the same physical quantity of much more efficient equipment.
13 An increase in the average size of the units of production, resulting in lower average costs.
14 A growth in employment in the secondary sector and a fall in employment in the primary sector.

15 This question is based on the information in the table below.

	Year 1		**Year 2**	
Country	**Output**	**Unemployment**	**Output**	**Unemployment**
A	100	5%	101	5%
B	100	5%	102	2%
C	100	5%	90	8%
D	100	5%	104	1%

Assuming no change in the size of the working population, which country has experienced an increase in its productive capacity?

True or false?

16 **a** Early economists saw the law of diminishing returns as a serious limitation on a country's potential for economic growth.
b Innovation is generally held to be a major source of economic growth.
c A growing population always acts as a brake on the rate of economic growth.
d A significant rise in the capital/output ratio indicates that technical progress has been an important contributor to the growth of output.
e The absence of an established infrastructure is a serious barrier to economic development.
f It is capital 'widening' rather than capital 'deepening' that is an important contributor to increased productivity.

Data response question

17 This question is based on the graph below.

Productivity growth and investment

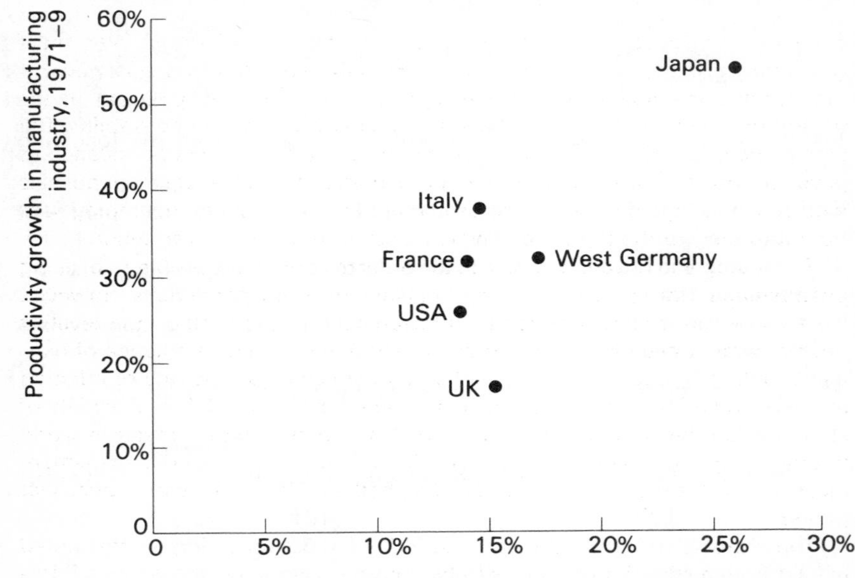

*Excludes house building

Source: *Barclays Bank Review*, August 1981

a Explain briefly the basic information contained in the graph.
b How would you account for the position of the UK relative to the positions of the other industrialised countries in the diagram?

Part 9

Managing the economy

For some two decades following the end of the Second World War, most governments in the industrialised non-communist world tended to use Keynesian demand management techniques (fiscal and monetary policies) in the pursuit of the main objectives of economic policy; namely, price stability, full employment, a satisfactory rate of economic growth and a sound balance of payments position. In general, during this period, demand management policies worked with a high degree of success, particularly in preventing unemployment from returning to the high levels which existed in the inter-war period.

The raising and lowering of demand in order to counter the problems of rising unemployment or rising inflation and balance of payments deficits, however, led to a series of stop–go cycles. Unfortunately, at each 'stop', the level of unemployment needed to slow down inflation and eliminate balance of payments deficits gradually became higher, and at each 'go', the rate of inflation accelerated and the balance of payments sank further into deficit. A variety of structural and institutional changes in the UK, together with changes in world trading conditions, made it increasingly difficult to apply demand management measures with the degree of success they had enjoyed in the earlier post-war period.

These problems were clearly acknowledged in the following much-quoted extract from a speech made in 1976 by James Callaghan when he was Prime Minister:

> We used to think that we could just spend our way out of a recession and increase employment by cutting taxes and boosting government spending. I tell you in all candour that that option no longer exists, and that in so far as it ever did exist, it worked by injecting inflation into the economy. And each time that happened, the average level of unemployment has risen. Higher inflation, followed by higher unemployment. That is the history of the last 20 years.

The problem of stagflation has led to a wide range of suggested policy changes, some of which are outlined briefly below.

1. A much greater degree of state control over the flow of and allocation of funds for investment (as a means of stimulating economic growth).
2. The use of import controls to reduce the leakages which follow increases in aggregate demand (and, of course, as a means of protecting UK industry).
3. A substantial depreciation of the pound in order to stimulate exports and discourage imports.
4. The introduction of an incomes policy supported by sanctions to make it

more effective (e.g. by penalising firms which increase pay by more than the norm).

5 The use of price controls to restrict inflation and to encourage the acceptance of a voluntary incomes policy.

6 Making the control of the money supply the main instrument of economic management and, by allowing it to grow at some given steady rate, to remove what monetarists see as the main cause of the stop–go cycles (i.e discretionary monetary policy).

Some of these measures are not intended as substitutes for the traditional demand management techniques; they are seen as necessary *supporting* measures.

Short answer questions

1 One of the monetarists' main arguments against the use of fiscal policy as an instrument for increasing aggregate demand is that it leads to 'crowding out'. What is meant by 'crowding out', and how is it supposed to arise?

2 Why would flat-rate increases in incomes be generally regarded as an unsuitable basis for a longer-term incomes policy?

3 'With a low level of unemployment, incomes policy will be ineffective; with a high level of unemployment, incomes policy is unnecessary.' Comment briefly on this observation.

4 Why is it desirable to incorporate some degree of flexibility into an incomes policy? Why is it difficult to operate an incomes policy which does contain a degree of flexibility?

5 'The abolition of exchange controls in 1979 tended to reduce the upward pressure on sterling.' Explain.

6 In discussions on the likely effectiveness of monetary policy as a means of stimulating the economy and of reducing inflationary pressures, it is sometimes observed that 'one can pull on a piece of string but one cannot push it'. Explain the relevance of this remark.

7 If the Chancellor of the Exchequer reduced public expenditure by £1000 million but at the same time reduced taxation by £1000 million, would the effect on national income be neutral? Explain your answer.

8 To which broad grouping of the instruments of economic policy does each of the following measures belong?

a a reduction in the PSBR
b an increase in investment grants
c a large-scale funding operation
d a managed depreciation of sterling
e the use of Industrial Development Certificates
f the introduction of a Restrictive Practices Court

9 Why is an increase of, say, 10 per cent in aggregate demand not likely to lead to an increase in employment of 10 per cent? Assume there are unemployed resources.

10 In the OECD countries, the number of jobs increased by 28 million in the 1970s, but unemployment continued to rise. Population growth was *one* of the reasons. What other factors might have accounted for this rise in unemployment?

11 It has been suggested that one cause of the higher unemployment rates in the 1970s was the combined effect of higher social security benefits and lower real tax thresholds which reduced the net financial gain from taking jobs. Therefore, it is said, people became more selective in job choice and spent more time on 'search' between jobs.
a What is the meaning and relevance of 'lower real tax thresholds'?
b Why should an extension of the average amount of time spent between jobs increase the numbers registered as unemployed (assuming the rates at which people are losing jobs and finding jobs remain the same)?

12 In what sense can the equilibrium level of national income be higher than the full employment level of national income?

Multiple choice questions

Questions **13**, **14**, and **15** are based on the following policy measures.

A the introduction of investment grants
B an increase in the general level of interest rates
C a reduction in government spending with a view to achieving a substantial Budget surplus
D a managed appreciation of the pound sterling

Other things being equal, which of the above measures will be most likely to
13 reduce the PSBR?
14 reduce the official foreign currency reserves?
15 stimulate economic growth?

16 Which of the following measures will *directly* increase the money supply?
1 intervention by the monetary authorities in the gilt-edged market to prevent a rise in interest rates
2 increased government sales of Treasury bills to the banking system
3 an instruction to the banks to maintain a greater degree of liquidity in the composition of their assets

A 1, 2, and 3
B 1 and 2 only
C 2 and 3 only
D 1 only
E 3 only

17 A substantial increase in the PSBR financed by borrowing from the non-bank private sector would tend to

1 increase the national debt.
2 lead to a rise in interest rates.
3 increase the money supply.

A 1, 2, and 3
B 1 and 2 only
C 2 and 3 only
D 1 only
E 3 only

18 Which of the following is/are major objectives of a policy of indexation?
1 to diminish the effects of inflation on the distribution of income
2 to reduce the extent of fiscal drag
3 to bring about an increase in real incomes

A 1, 2, and 3
B 1 and 2 only
C 2 and 3 only
D 1 only
E 3 only

19 An open economy with a government sector and unemployed resources is in equilibrium. Other things being equal, the effect of an increase in exports will be
1 a fall in the external value of the currency.
2 an increase in tax revenue.
3 an increase in employment.

A 1, 2, and 3
B 1 and 2 only
C 2 and 3 only
D 1 only
E 3 only

20 Which of the following policies is a government likely to adopt if it wishes to reduce demand-pull inflationary pressures at home *and* to eliminate or reduce a balance of payments surplus?
1 revaluation
2 increasing the average rate of tariff on its imports
3 lowering the rate of interest

A 1, 2, and 3
B 1 and 2 only
C 2 and 3 only
D 1 only
E 3 only

True or false?

21 **a** Devaluation and tariffs both make use of the price mechanism as a means of restricting imports.
b Interest rate changes act on the demand for credit while a call for (or repayment of) special deposits acts on the supply of money.
c Export-led growth is a misnomer because an increase in exports reduces the domestic supply of goods.
d If there is a substantial amount of excess capacity in the economy, devaluation will only be successful if it is accompanied by a deflationary policy.
e The main purpose of an incomes policy is to ensure that incomes rise at the same rate as prices.
f Monetarists argue that a discretionary monetary policy is destabilising.
g If the growth of GDP slows down more than productivity does, employment will start to fall.

Data response questions

22 You are given the following information about an economy:
1 There are no transactions with the rest of the world.
2 The MPS of households is one-fifth of disposable income and is constant.
3 The only tax is a proportionate income tax at the rate of 20 per cent.
4 Initially the economy is in equilibrium with planned investment equal to £5000m. and government spending on goods and services equal to £4000m.
5 The government now increases its expenditure to £5800m. while investment and the rate of taxation remain unchanged.
a What was the initial level of income?
b What is the value of the multiplier?
c What is the new equilibrium level of income following the increase in government spending?
d What is the amount by which consumption increases as a result of the increase in income?
e What is the Budget surplus or deficit in new equilibrium situation?

23 The question is based on the quotations and diagram that follow. The quotations refer to events following the two very large increases in the price of oil, 1973–4 and 1979–80.

> Both oil price shocks exerted a sharp deflationary impulse on the world economy. Each shock resulted in a reduction of real income of about 2% of GDP to the industrial world.

> In the period immediately after the second oil shock, prices increased swiftly, almost doubling between the middle of 1978 and 1979 while

earnings rose more slowly and by less. The slower growth of nominal wages relative to prices compared with the aftermath of the first oil shock, reflects, in large part, the non-accommodating economic policies adopted by most governments.

*Earnings and inflation in nine major economies** (*percentage changes on the same quarter a year earlier*)

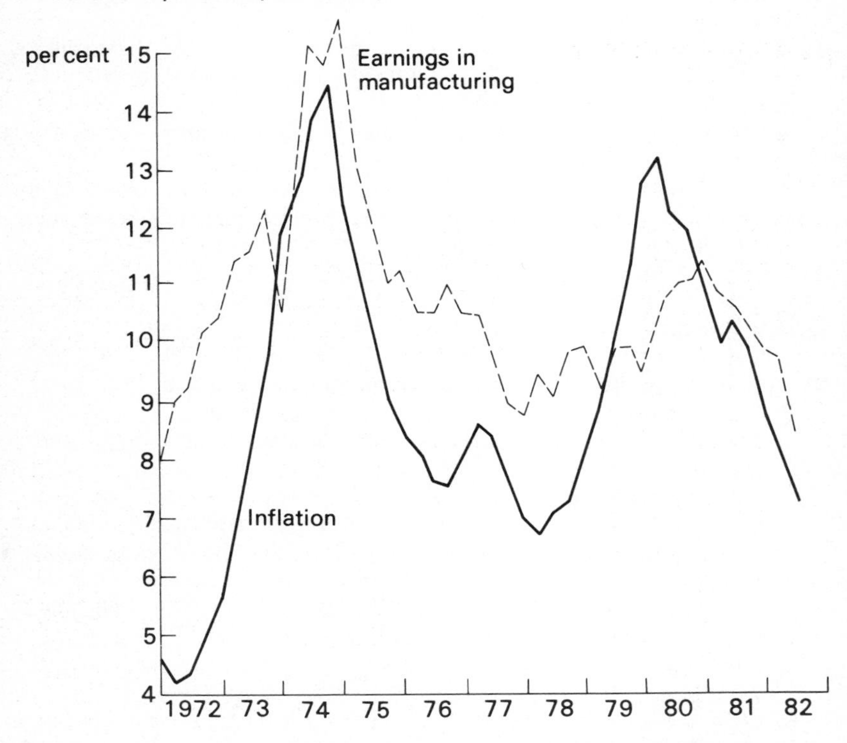

*Belgium, Canada, France, Germany (FR), Holland, Italy, Japan, UK, USA

Source: *Economic Progress Report*, HMSO, January 1983

a (1st extract) The diagram shows a very sharp increase in the rate of inflation following each of the large increases in the price of oil. How then can it be said that the increased oil prices 'exerted a sharp deflationary impulse to the world economy'? Explain how the increase in oil prices reduced real income in the industrial world.
b (2nd extract) Explain why the slower growth of nominal wages relative to prices was due to non-accommodating economic policies.
c What happened to the real earnings of those employed in manufacturing in 1981–2?

Answers

Answers to part 1

Short answer questions

1 GNP at market prices includes the effect on prices of indirect taxes and subsidies, whereas GNP at factor cost measures the value of expenditure net of taxes and subsidies. Without the adjustment to factor cost, therefore, it would be possible to change the 'market value' of a given flow of output (and hence national income) simply by changing the rates of taxation and the level of subsidies.

2 Transfer payments are forms of income which are not payments for services rendered; they simply involve a redistribution of income within the community. They must be distinguished from other government expenditures which involve the purchase of goods and services, because these latter expenditures are payments for services rendered and add directly to the national income.

3 National income = Total personal disposable income
minus Transfer payments
plus Direct taxes (including national insurance contributions)
plus Undistributed profits of companies and surpluses of public corporations

4 Net property income from abroad might be positive or negative. If it is positive, GNP > GDP; if it is negative, GNP < GDP.

5 From total domestic expenditure we must *subtract* (i) expenditure on imports, (ii) property income paid abroad, (iii) taxes on goods and services and (iv) depreciation, and *add* (i) total export earnings, (ii) property income received from abroad and (iii) subsidies.

6 Some resources owned by UK residents, such as foreign subsidiaries of UK companies, are located overseas. These resources generate income, part of which is remitted to the UK in the form of interest, profits and dividends. This income is included in the national income of the UK since it represents a claim on the output of other countries. Similarly, foreign-owned enterprises located in the UK remit some of their earnings to their home countries. Net property income from abroad represents the difference between these flows of income. It can be positive or negative.

7 If gross investment is insufficient to cover the depreciation on existing assets, net investment will be negative. In such a case, the country is said to be consuming its capital.

8 The income, output and expenditure methods of measuring the national income should, in theory, produce the same total. In practice, the available information is not accurate or comprehensive enough to ensure this, so the measured flows of income and output are adjusted by a residual error in order to make them equal to the measured expenditure flow. This does not imply that expenditure is a better measure of national income.

9 Nominal GNP is simply the money value of GNP. The real value of GNP for any given year cannot be measured in terms of money because it consists of the volumes of the different goods and services produced, and these physical quantities cannot be aggregated. By expressing the values of GNP for different years at constant prices, however, *changes* in real GNP can be estimated. By expressing the value of output in year 2 in terms of the prices ruling in year 1, we can estimate the movement in the volume of output between year 1 and year 2.

10 The following are included: **b**, **d**, **e**, **f**, **g**, **h**, **i** and **j**.

11 Consumption creates a demand for, and generates income for, the factors of production. It does not diminish the stock of the factors of production. Capital consumption (depreciation), on the other hand, means that part of the capital stock is being *used up* in the production processes. It tends, therefore, to reduce the stock of productive assets.

12 Owner-occupied dwellings are classed as part of the nation's stock of productive capital because they produce a flow of services to their owners. The value of these services (i.e. the estimated rent the houses would earn if let) must be *imputed* into the national income. A failure to impute a value for these services would create the anomalous situation where the national income would fall if more families bought their own homes.

13 Income would still equal output because the unanticipated fall in the value of output would be matched by an unanticipated fall in the income accruing to the entrepreneur (i.e. profits).

14 Double counting occurs when items of output are counted more than once. For example, if both the total output of the steel industry and the total output of the car industry are counted, then the steel content of the cars will be counted twice. Double counting can be avoided by (i) only counting the value added at each stage of production or (ii) only counting the value of the final products.

15 **a** Total domestic expenditure at market prices = £208 000 million
b Total final expenditure at market prices = £253 000 million
c Gross Domestic Product at market prices = £213 000 million
d Gross National Product at market prices = £212 950 million
e Gross National Product at factor cost = £162 950 million
f National income = £132 950 million

16 Transactions are concealed when income is not reported to the authorities. Some of this under-reporting will involve legal untaxed transactions (e.g. if two persons render services to one another on a barter basis), but some will arise from the deliberate under-statement of income to evade tax.

17 One way in which the size of the 'hidden economy' can be estimated is by subtracting recorded incomes from recorded expenditures. This is not entirely satisfactory since income earned in the hidden economy might also be spent in the hidden economy or saved. The existence of the hidden economy certainly makes national income statistics less accurate as a true measure of the level of output. So long as national income is estimated in the same way each year, however, the *trends* should be reasonably reliable.

18 The national income in year 10, measured at year 1 prices is

$$£75\,000 \text{ million} \times \frac{100}{125} = £60\,000 \text{ million}$$

Real national income, therefore, has increased by 20 per cent.

19 **a** The GNP at market prices is 1250 currency units.
b The national income is 1100 currency units.

Multiple choice questions

20 C **21** B **22** B **23** E **24** E **25** D **26** B **27** B **28** C
29 B

True or false?

30 **a** True **b** False **c** False **d** True **e** True **f** True **g** False
h False **i** False

Data response questions

31 **a** (i) £146 079 million
(ii) £210 921 million
(iii) £47 726 million

b During inflation, the monetary value of stocks held will increase. The national income, however, is an attempt to measure the value of real output during the course of one year. For this reason, only the value of the *real* (or physical) increase in stocks can be recorded.

c The additional information required is an indication of the extent to which prices have changed. This is provided by an index of prices which can be used to measure real changes in GDP (see the answer to question **18**).

d Total investment = Fixed investment *plus* Additions to stocks
= £39 377m. − £4160m.
= £35 217m.

e The main reason was falling demand as the economy moved deeper into recession. The fall in demand discouraged entrepreneurs from undertaking expenditures on new fixed assets and encouraged them to reduce their holdings of stocks; hence the reduction in total investment. Cutting back on production and running down stocks is one way in which a firm can bring about an immediate (but not a long-run) improvement in its financial position.

32 **a** GDP refers to the value of the total output produced by resources located in the UK. In order to measure GDP at constant factor cost, it is necessary to make two important adjustments to the value of GDP at market prices:
(i) It is necessary to deduct indirect taxes and add on subsidies in order to obtain the value of output at factor cost.
(ii) In order to remove the effects of inflation it is necessary to make use of an index number of prices so as to deflate the monetary value of GDP (see the answer to question **18**).
b Since changes in living standards are very dependent on movements in real income, changes in GDP at constant factor cost should provide a reasonably good guide to movements in the general standard of living. There are, however, several important determinants of the standard of living which are not revealed by the information in the graph:
(i) Changes in living standards are influenced by changes in GNP rather than GDP, but the difference between these two aggregates (i.e. net property income from abroad) is relatively small as far as the UK is concerned.
(ii) While the graph illustrates the movements in *total* domestic output, it is movements in GDP *per capita* that are relevant to estimates of changes in living standards. Over the period under discussion, however, the changes in the UK population would not significantly affect GDP per capita.
(iii) The general standard of living depends very much on the distribution of GDP. Over the period 1979–82, there may well have been changes in the distribution of real income. This was a period of rapidly increasing unemployment. While the average standard of living may well have fallen, the burden of this fall was not shared evenly. Those who lost their jobs suffered a fall in living standards while those in work may well have experienced some increase in their standard of living (average earnings rose by 60 per cent, while prices rose by 51 per cent).
(iv) Another factor which has a bearing on the relationship between GDP and living standards is the composition of GDP (i.e. the variety of goods and services produced). Although there was a small increase in defence spending, the level of investment spending (at constant prices) fell over this period. The proportion of GDP made up of consumption goods, therefore, would have changed little.
(v) Living standards, of course, are influenced by such things as the amount of leisure and the supply and quality of the various social services available to the people. Over the relatively short period under consideration, these features are unlikely to have changed in any significant manner.

Given the fact that many of the other important determinants of living standards will have changed very little during the period 1979–82, it would be reasonable to assume that the average standard of living in the UK did fall.

33 a Gross investment = Output of capital goods *plus* Imports

minus Exports of capital goods	£170m.
Additions to stocks	£20m.
Change in overseas assets	0
	£190m.

b

Stock of consumer goods at beginning of year	£30m.
Output of consumer goods	£150m.
Imports of consumer goods *minus* Exports of consumer goods	£20m.
	£200m.
minus Stock of consumer goods at end of year	−£50m.
Total consumption	£150m.

c Since there is no property income paid abroad or received from abroad, GNP is given by the sum of gross investment and total consumption.

Gross investment	£190m.
Total consumption	£150m.
Gross National Product	£340m.

d

Gross National Product	£340m.
less Depreciation	−£19m.
National income	£321m.

Answers to part 2

Short answer questions

1 **a** C^1
b C^2

2 The level of disposable real income is the main factor since this determines the ability to spend. Disposable real income depends upon the level of total real income and the rates at which income is taxed. But there are several other factors that can change consumption independently of changes in total disposable real income. Some of these are:
(i) Changes in the distribution of income. If households have different MPCs, a redistribution of income will change the level of consumption spending. Income may be redistributed by means of direct taxation and government expenditures on transfer payments.
(ii) Expectations regarding future price changes.
(iii) Variations in the terms on which credit may be obtained. The availability and cost of credit is an important determinant of the demand for many durable consumer goods.
(iv) Expectations of future changes in income.

3 When income is relatively low and people are so poor that they can only afford the bare necessities of life, saving is impossible. As income increases, people can purchase commodities which make life more enjoyable but are not absolutely essential, and it becomes possible to save. As the standard of living rises further (due to rising real income), the urgency of unsatisfied wants becomes less and less, and hence less sacrifice is involved in saving.

4 The marginal propensity to consume of an economy is greater than *zero* but less than *unity* for all levels of income.

5 A negative MPC would imply that consumption falls as income rises. Empirical evidence demonstrates that this does not happen.

6 (i) a is a constant which indicates that consumption will be positive even when disposable income is zero.
(ii) b is also a constant and represents the proportion of disposable income devoted to consumption at all levels of disposable income.

7 In this type of economy, any increase in income must either be spent or saved. Thus the proportion spent plus the proportion saved must equal 1.

8 If consumption is related to total real income then those 'other things' refer to changes in the taxation of income and in the various factors set out in the answer to question **2**.

9 A large part of personal saving is contractual in the sense that individuals enter into agreements to save regular amounts. Examples include insurance premiums, contributions to pension funds and various savings schemes run by the building societies and SAYE.

10 The major forms of saving are (i) personal contractual saving (see the answer to question **9**), (ii) company saving which is carried out for the purpose of building up reserves for further investment and (iii) government saving (i.e. a Budget surplus) which is carried out for purposes of economic policy (e.g. to reduce aggregate demand in the economy). The motives for these forms of saving are such that most of this saving is not likely to be significantly affected by changes in the rate of interest.

11 At relatively low levels of income, consumption may be financed by past savings (or a country may borrow abroad). This is referred to as dissavings.

12

Y	*C*	*S*	*APC*	*MPC*	*APS*	*MPS*
1000	1500	−500	1.5	—	−0.5	—
2000	2400	−400	1.2	0.9	−0.2	0.1
3000	3150	−150	1.05	0.75	−0.05	0.25
4000	3600	400	0.9	0.45	0.1	0.55
5000	4000	1000	0.8	0.4	0.2	0.6
6000	4200	1800	0.7	0.2	0.3	0.8

Note: The values of *Y*, *C* and *S* are in £ million.

13 Initially, as a proportion of total income,

$$C = 0.75 \times 0.8Y$$
$$= 0.6Y$$

After increase in tax,

$$C = 0.75 \times 0.6Y$$
$$= 0.45Y$$

14 **a** A movement to C^2.
b A movement to C^1.
c A movement to C^1.
d A movement to C^2.

15 A pound that will be earned next year is worth less than a pound earned now, if only because the latter could be loaned for a year and thus gain interest. It should also be apparent that a sum of money which is immediately available is 'worth more' than the same sum of money due for payment in one or two years' time.

If the rate of interest is 10 per cent, a deposit of £100 will be worth £110 in one year's time. Thus we can say that when the rate of interest is 10 per cent, the present value of £110 due in one year's time is £100. In more precise terms, when the rate of interest is 10 per cent, the present value of £110 due in one year is

$$\frac{£110}{1+r} = \frac{£110}{1.1} = £100$$

where r is the rate of interest, i.e. 10/100.

If the £110 is due in two years' time, its present value is

$$\frac{£110}{(1+r)^2} = \frac{£110}{(1.1)^2} = £90.9$$

16 **a** The marginal efficiency of capital is one way of expressing the marginal productivity of capital. It is the rate at which a flow of expected receipts from the employment of some new investment must be discounted so that the discounted value of these expected returns exactly equals the supply price of the asset.

b If the supply of the other factors remains constant and the supply of capital increases, the marginal productivity of capital is likely to fall because of diminishing returns to the variable factor (capital). The increased supply of the product is also likely to lower its price. Both of these factors will reduce the expected revenues from additional investment.

17

	Demand for product (units)	Number of machines				
		Existing stock	Required stock	Replacement demand	Net investment	Total investment
Year 1	10000	50	50	5	0	5
Year 2	12000	50	60	5	10	15

The 20 per cent increase in the demand for consumer goods has created a 200 per cent increase in the demand for capital goods.

This example assumes that the industry in question would react in the manner shown. It might, however, consider the increase in demand to be only temporary and would then tend to lengthen its order books rather than commit itself to an increase in its capital stock.

18 The values used in the calculations (for example, those used in calculating the present value of expected future earnings) are based on estimates of future revenues and future costs. There is no way of predicting future events with any degree of certainty. Hence there is a very large element of intelligent guesswork, particularly in making decisions about long-term investment.

Multiple choice questions

19 A **20** D **21** C **22** C **23** B **24** E

True or false?

25 **a** False **b** True **c** False **d** True **e** True **f** False **g** True **h** True

Data response questions

26 **a** We use the current rate of interest to discount the expected future returns in the following manner.

$$\text{Present value} = \frac{£1500}{1.05} + \frac{£1450}{(1.05)^2} + \frac{£1350}{(1.05)^3} + \frac{£1150}{(1.05)^4} + \frac{£900}{(1.05)^5}$$

$$\approx £5561$$

b The calculations show that this investment project would be profitable. We must bear in mind, however, that the returns used in the calculation are *expected* returns (see the answer to question **18**). Unforeseen changes in the demand for the product, the rate of interest, the cost of production and the rate of depreciation (due to technical progress) might cause the project to be far more profitable or far less profitable than the initial estimates indicated.

c It would reduce the present value of the expected returns to

$$\frac{£1500}{1.1} + \frac{£1450}{(1.1)^2} + \frac{£1350}{(1.1)^3} + \frac{£1150}{(1.1)^4} + \frac{£900}{(1.1)^5} \approx £4921$$

On the basis of this calculation, and given the great uncertainty involved in the estimates, it is most unlikely that the firm would proceed with the project.

27 **a** Total personal savings consists of saving by households but also includes saving by sole proprietors and partnerships, private trusts and non-profitmaking bodies such as charities. The main forms taken by personal savings are: (i) life assurance and pension funds, (ii) building society deposits, (iii) bank deposits and (iv) national savings.

b For many years the conventional wisdom was that since inflation represented an erosion in the value of money it would act as a deterrent to saving. Recent experience seems to demonstrate that the opposite is true. Much of the wealth held by individuals is in the form of building society deposits, bank deposits and national savings certificates which are fixed in money terms. Inflation acts to reduce the real value of these assets and individuals may have attempted to restore the real value of their savings by saving more.

Rising unemployment may have induced people to save more against the greater risk of becoming unemployed. But those who lost their jobs saved a very much smaller proportion of their income than they did when in work. Analysis shows that this latter effect predominated so that high unemployment tended to reduce the savings ratio.

The 1970s was a decade associated with historically high interest rates. Again, these high interest rates might have been expected to stimulate saving. In fact, the *real* rate of interest was very low during this period and for some of the time it was negative.

One factor which might have had a positive effect on the savings ratio was the fact that the slowing down of the growth of real income, rising unemployment and fears about the effects of anti-inflationary policies made people much less optimistic about future incomes and hence persuaded them to save more.

The main influence, however, appears to have been the effects of inflation on the level of wealth held by individuals and their desire to maintain the real value of their savings.

Answers to part 3

1 The two-sector economy

Short answer questions

1 Realised investment = Planned investment + Unplanned investment

a Realised investment, therefore, will exceed planned investment when there is a fall in demand and an unplanned increase in stocks.

b Planned investment will exceed realised investment when aggregate demand exceeds the planned output of firms. This excess demand will cause an unplanned running-down of stocks. Unplanned investment, therefore, will be a negative quantity.

2 Income is in equilibrium when producers and consumers have no incentive to change their behaviour; income is stable. The necessary condition is that aggregate output (income) equals aggregate demand. For a two-sector economy, this means that

$$Y = C + I$$

Alternatively we may say that an economy is in equilibrium when planned injections are equal to planned leakages, which, for a two-sector economy, means

$$\text{Planned } I = \text{Planned } S$$

3 The immediate effect of an increase in the rate of saving will be an increase in unplanned investment (i.e. an increase in stocks due to the fall in demand). The longer-term effect will probably be a fall in planned investment as firms react to the fall in demand.

4 If other things remain equal, an increase in planned saving implies a reduction in planned consumption. In response to this, firms will reduce their outputs and the consequent fall in income will result in a fall in saving. This is referred to as the paradox of thrift.

5 a $\text{Multiplier} = \dfrac{1}{\text{MPS}} = \dfrac{1}{0.25} = 4$

Therefore, $\Delta Y = 4 \times \Delta I = 200$

Equilibrium $Y = 1000$

b $C = 0.75Y = 750$

c $S = 0.25Y = 250$

6 In equilibrium

Planned S = Planned I

Therefore, in equilibrium, planned saving must be equal to £1000 million. This level of planned saving is attained when Y is £5000 million.

7 a The first three terms of the series enable us to deduce that the MPS is 0.4 and the MPC is 0.6. Thus, the successive increments in income and saving will be as follows.

$$\Delta Y = £5000\text{m.} + £3000\text{m.} + £1800\text{m.} + £1080\text{m.} + £648\text{m.} + \ldots$$
$$\Delta S = £2000\text{m.} + £1200\text{m.} + £720\text{m.} + £432\text{m.} + \ldots$$

b $$\Delta Y = \frac{1}{\text{MPS}} \times \Delta I$$

$$= \frac{1}{0.4} \times £5000\text{m.}$$

$$= £12\,500\text{m.}$$

8 Unplanned investment occurs when aggregate spending is insufficient to purchase aggregate output. In response to unplanned additions to stocks, firms will cut their outputs and hence income will fall.

9 This question may be answered by making use of the graph on p. 27. The eventual increase in income will be equal to the increase in investment spending plus the total increase in consumption spending (i.e. the sum of the increments in C). Clearly, the larger the MPC, the larger the increments in C and, hence, the greater is the multiplier effect.

10 a Equilibrium requires that aggregate supply is equal to aggregate demand,

i.e. $Y = C + I$

Therefore, equilibrium exists when

$$Y = £500\text{m.} + 0.8Y + £1500\text{m.}$$
$$0.2Y = £2000\text{m.}$$
$$Y = £10\,000\text{m.}$$

Alternatively, equilibrium exists when

$$\text{Planned } I = \text{Planned } S$$
i.e. when $$£1500\text{m.} = 0.2Y - £500\text{m.}$$
$$0.2Y = £2000\text{m.}$$
$$Y = £10\,000\text{m.}$$

b $$\text{Multiplier} = \frac{1}{\text{MPS}} = \frac{1}{0.2} = 5$$

11 When the propensity to consume increases, the propensity to save falls. Initially, therefore, the increase in C will be accompanied by a fall in S. But the increase in C will (via the multiplier) raise the level of income. Saving will gradually increase until it is once again equal to the (constant) value of investment.

12 **a** When *I* increases by £1000 million, consumption and saving begin to change as follows.

	C	***S***
Round 1	£800m.	£200m.
Round 2	£640m.	£160m.
Round 3	£512m.	£128m.

b Multiplier $= \dfrac{1}{1 - \text{MPC}} = \dfrac{1}{1 - 0.8} = 5$

13 What is true for an individual is not necessarily true for the whole community. See the answer to question **4** for an explanation of the consequences of a planned increase in *S* in the community.

Multiple choice questions

14 C **15** E **16** D **17** D **18** A **19** A **20** A **21** D **22** C **23** D

True or false?

24 **a** False **b** True **c** False **d** True **e** True **f** True **g** False

Data response questions

25

	Income	**Con-sumption**	**Saving**	**Planned investment**	**Unplanned investment**	**Realised investment**
Period 1	2000	1700	300	300	0	300
Period 2	2000	1600	400	300	100	400
Period 3	1900	1525	375	300	75	375
Period *N*	1600	1300	300	300	0	300

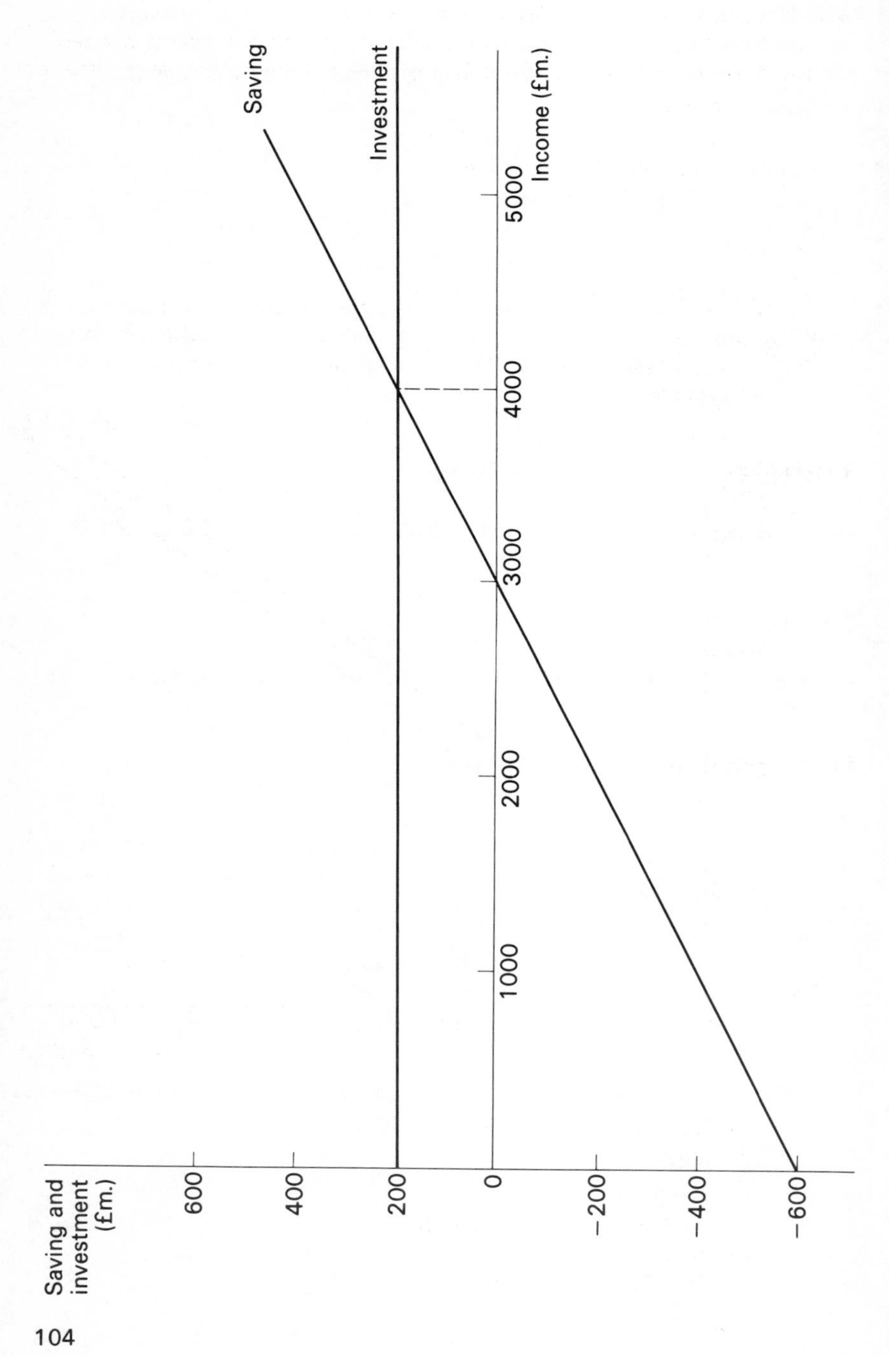
Saving and investment (£m.)
600
400
200
0
−200
−400
−600
1000
2000
3000
4000
5000
Income (£m.)
Saving
Investment

26 a The graph obtained is shown opposite.

From the graph, planned saving is equal to planned investment when income equals £4000 million. This is the equilibrium level of income.

b $C = Y - S$

$S = -600 + 0.2 \times £4000\text{m.} = £200\text{m.}$

Therefore $C = £4000\text{m.} - £200\text{m.}$

$= £3800\text{m.}$

c Multiplier $= \dfrac{1}{\text{MPS}} = \dfrac{1}{0.2} = 5$

d To draw this graph, derive the consumption function as follows:

$C = Y - S$
$= Y - (-600 + 0.25Y)$
$= 600 + 0.75Y$

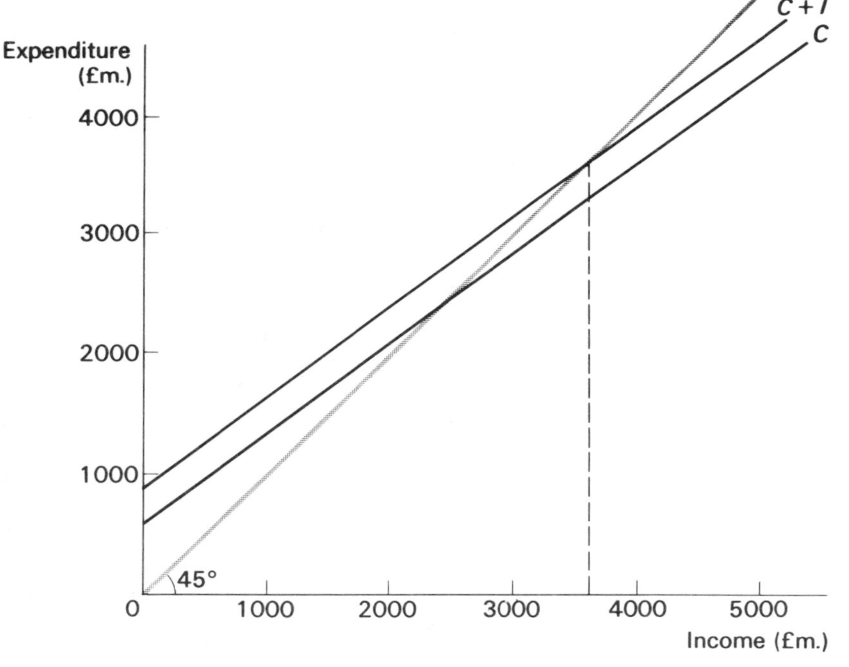

The $C + I$ line intersects the 45° line where income equals £3600 million. This is the equilibrium level of income.

Alternatively, in equilibrium,

$$Y = C + I$$
$$= £600\text{m.} + 0.75Y + £300\text{m.}$$
$$0.25Y = £900\text{m.}$$
$$Y = £3600\text{m.}$$

2 The three-sector economy

Short answer questions

1 It is an incorrect statement. Equilibrium in a two-sector economy requires that

$$S + T = I + G$$

It is not necessary, therefore, that G equals T.

2 Transfer payments merely redistribute income. The *spending* of transfer payments by households does create demand, but this appears as a component of C.

3 The multiplier is equal to the reciprocal of the marginal rate of *leakage* (or *withdrawal*).

4 The increase in G will lead to an expansionary multiplier process, the first term of which will be £1000 million. The increase in T will also lead to an expansionary multiplier process as private expenditure increases. However, some of the increase in disposable income will be saved, so the initial increase in private spending will be less than £1000 million. The multiplier process brought about by the reduction in T will have a first term equal to MPC × £1000 million.

5 Taxation is a leakage from the circular flow of income, and the smaller the rate of the leakage, the larger the multiplier.

6 A progressive tax reduces the rate of growth of disposable income when national income is increasing and allows disposable income to fall at a slower rate than gross income when national income is falling. Social security benefits will increase when output and factor incomes are falling, but they will fall when output and factor incomes are increasing. In both cases the effect is to reduce the severity of economic fluctuations.

7 Before the Second World War, it was generally believed that the Budget should be based on 'good housekeeping principles', and that expenditure should not exceed income. The work of Lord Keynes led to a general acceptance of the view that the Budget should be used to eliminate inflationary and deflationary gaps arising from discrepancies between the private sector's planned spending and the value of a full employment output.

8 If the debt is held by a relatively small percentage of the population and the tax payments are derived from taxes levied on a large percentage of the population, the inequality in the distribution of income will increase. The interest payments will represent a flow of income from 'the many' to 'the few'.

9 *Floating debt* is the debt which is financed by the issue of short-term securities (Treasury bills). *Internal debt* is that part of the national debt held (in the form of government securities) by residents of the country. *External debt* is that part of the national debt held by overseas residents.

10 **a** The $C+I+G$ line would move downwards because the fall in disposable income would reduce demand.

b The $C+I+G$ line would move upwards because the balanced budget multiplier is one (i.e. aggregate demand would increase by an amount equal to ΔG).

The increase in G would set up an expansionary multiplier process, the first term of which would be equal to ΔG. The increase in T would lead to a contractionary process, the first term of which would be less than ΔT (because the increase in T would reduce saving as well as spending). In other words, the increase in demand due to the increase in G would be greater than the fall in demand due to the increase in T.

11 It will be regressive if it is placed on commodities widely consumed by all income groups. The element of taxation in the price of the commodity will account for a greater proportion of the incomes of the lower income groups.

12 **a** The equilibrium level of income will fall.

b The total value of $S+T$ will also fall.

13 $\text{MPS} = 0.2 \times 0.75Y = 0.15Y$

$\text{MRT} = 0.25Y$

$$\text{Multiplier} = \frac{1}{\text{MPS}+\text{MRT}} = \frac{1}{0.15+0.25} = \frac{1}{0.4} = 2.5$$

14 The opportunity cost of building a motorway is the alternative output which the resources used in the construction of the motorway might have produced. They might, for example, have been used to construct houses, schools, hospitals, docks, airports and so on. These alternatives are forgone by the community at the time the motorway is built. In this particular sense, therefore, the real cost is not passed on. In fact, future generations might be regarded as beneficiaries in the sense that they will inherit a larger stock of real capital.

Multiple choice questions

15 A **16** C **17** E **18** D **19** C

True or false?

20 **a** False **b** False **c** True **d** False **e** True **f** False **g** True **h** False **i** True **j** True

Data response questions

21 **a** The CGBR represents the total borrowing requirement by the central government. A part of this borrowing will be required for its own purposes (i.e. £8.5 billion) while part of the government's borrowing will be for re-lending to local authorities and the public corporations (i.e. £3.0 billion). Local authorities are expected to use this borrowing from the central government to repay some of their borrowings from the non-public sector. To the extent that these debts are repaid, public sector debt will be reduced by £0.2 billion. The public corporations are also expected to use money borrowed from the central government to repay some of their loans from lenders other than the central government, but they will still be net borrowers to the extent of £1.1 billion. The 'unallocated item' refers to expected 'gains' which will serve to reduce the public sector borrowing requirement.

b The PSBR is financed by various types of borrowing:
(i) by sales of different types of securities such as long-term government securities, Treasury bills, and local authority bonds and bills, to members of the non-bank public,
(ii) national savings,
(iii) borrowing from the banking system and
(iv) borrowing from overseas residents.

22 **a** A major cause of the large rise in the total interest payments was the fact that interest rates were at relatively high levels during the period discussed in the quotation. In 1966 the highest rate on any government stock was 6%. In the succeeding seven-year period some securities were issued bearing interest rates as high as 15%.

b Some of the funds borrowed by the public sector are converted into income-earning assets. Borrowings by local authorities may be used to build houses which yield income in the form of rent. Public corporations use borrowed funds to purchase capital assets (e.g. power stations, gas pipelines and telephone exchanges) which yield a trading income. Some government borrowing is also on-lent to firms in the private sector in the form of interest-bearing loans. A part of the *gross debt interest* which the public sector has to pay, therefore, is paid for by receipts of 'trading' income or by interest from outside the public sector. *Net interest* consists of those interest payments which are a charge on taxation or which necessitate further government borrowing.

c The 'real' cost of interest charges would have risen by less than the nominal cost because of the relatively high rates of inflation during the period under discussion. In fact, for a short period, the real rate of interest was negative. In 1982–3, however, the fairly rapid fall in inflation was accompanied by a much slower fall in interest rates and the real rate of interest was relatively high.

d Interest payments on public sector debt are treated as transfer payments and do not contribute *directly* to aggregate demand. Public spending on education, health and transport constitutes a demand for goods and services and adds directly to aggregate demand.

3 The four-sector economy

Short answer questions

1 When a country reduces its imports, it has the effect of reducing the national income in those countries whose exports have been reduced. A fall in income usually leads to a lower level of imports. This income effect, therefore, is likely to have adverse effects on the exports of the country which has deliberately reduced its imports. There might also be some form of retaliation by the countries whose exports have been restricted.

2 Exports are an injection into the circular flow of income because they represent a demand for the national product which is *additional* to the demands from domestic firms and households.

3

$$Y_d = \tfrac{3}{4}Y$$
$$\therefore C = \tfrac{2}{3} \times \tfrac{3}{4}Y = \tfrac{1}{2}Y$$
$$\therefore M = \tfrac{1}{5} \times \tfrac{1}{2}Y = \tfrac{1}{10}Y$$
$$\text{MPS} = \tfrac{1}{3} \times \tfrac{3}{4}Y = \tfrac{1}{4}Y$$
$$\text{MRT} = \tfrac{1}{4}Y$$
$$\text{MPM} = \tfrac{1}{10}Y$$

$$\text{Multiplier} = \frac{1}{\text{MPS} + \text{MRT} + \text{MPM}} = \frac{1}{\frac{1}{4} + \frac{1}{4} + \frac{1}{10}} = 1.66$$

4 a

$$Y_d = 0.8Y$$
$$\therefore \text{APC} = 0.75 \times 0.8Y = 0.6Y$$

Equilibrium exists when

$$Y = C + I + G + X - M$$

i.e. when

$$Y = 0.6Y + £1250\text{m.} + £1500\text{m.} + £750\text{m.} - 0.3Y$$
$$0.7Y = £3500\text{m.}$$
$$Y = £5000 \text{ million}$$

b $G = £1500$ million

$T = 0.2 \times £5000\text{m.} = £1000$ million

There is a Budget *deficit* of £500 million.

c $X = £750\text{m.}$

$M = 0.3 \times £5000\text{m.} = £1500\text{m.}$

There is a balance of payments *deficit* of £750 million.

5 Assuming the rates of leakage are constant,

$$\text{MRT} = \tfrac{1}{10}Y$$
$$\text{MPS} = \tfrac{1}{9} \times \tfrac{9}{10}Y = \tfrac{1}{10}Y$$
$$\text{MPM} = \tfrac{1}{8} \times \tfrac{8}{9} \times \tfrac{9}{10}Y = \tfrac{1}{10}Y$$

$$\text{MRT} + \text{MPS} + \text{MPM} = \tfrac{3}{10}Y$$
$$\therefore \quad \text{MPC} = \tfrac{7}{10}Y$$
Hence $\Delta Y = -£500\text{m.} - £350\text{m.} - £245\text{m.} - \ldots$

Multiple choice questions

6 D **7** D **8** B **9** E **10** C **11** C **12** C

True or false?

13 **a** True **b** False **c** False **d** True **e** False **f** False **g** True **h** True

Data response questions

14 **a** (i)

Increase in GDP	£1000m.
Retained profits plus corporation tax	£150m.
Increase in personal income	£850m.
Direct taxation	£272m.
Increase in personal disposable income	£578m.

(ii) Increase in consumer spending at market prices

= 75% of £578m. = £433.5m.

(iii)

Increase in consumer spending at market prices	£433.5m.
Indirect taxes less subsidies	£65.0m.
Increase in consumer spending at factor cost	£368.5m. (app.)
Import content	£73.7m.
Increase in consumer spending on domestic output at factor cost	£294.8m. (app.)

b $\text{MPC} = \dfrac{294.8}{1000} = 0.2948$

$$\text{Multiplier} = \frac{1}{1 - 0.2948} \approx 1.33$$

15 a Households' income = 1600 + 200

Households' income = 1600 + 200	1800
less Saving + Imports + Direct taxes	400
Consumer spending on domestic output at market prices	1400
Less Expenditure taxes	200
Consumer spending on domestic output at factor cost	1200

b Using the expenditure method,

$$\begin{aligned} GNP &= C + I + G + X - M \\ &= 1200 + 300 + 500 + 250 - 200 \\ &= 2050 \end{aligned}$$

Note: The deduction for imports is only 200 because the value for C (1200) is expressed net of import content (and expenditure taxes).

c The income generated by firms is disposed of in the following manner:

Factor incomes paid to households (1600) + Retained profits (100) + Direct taxation (150) + Expenditure on imports (200) = 2050

This is exactly equal to aggregate demand (see the answer to part **b**).
Alternatively,

Planned injections $(I + G + X) = 300 + 500 + 250 = 1050$
Planned leakages $(S + T + M) = 200 + 550 + 300 = 1050$

Since planned leakages are equal to planned injections, the economy is in equilibrium.

d The consumption of domestic output at factor cost is 1200. If rates of withdrawal remain constant,

$$APC = MPC = \frac{1200}{2050} = 0.585$$

$$\text{Multiplier} = \frac{1}{1 - 0.585} \approx 2.4$$

Answers to part 4

Short answer questions

1 Money is a completely liquid asset and its *money value* is certain. The money value of other assets is uncertain. The disadvantages are that money earns no income and, during periods of inflation, its exchange value falls.

2 This is best explained by an example. If a hunter wishes to exchange his pelts for corn, he must find someone who has a surplus of corn *and* who also requires pelts.

3 **a** A fiduciary issue of banknotes is one which is not backed by precious metal (usually gold). Such note issues are invariably backed by government securities.

b Legal tender refers to those forms of money which must be accepted in the discharge of debts. In the UK, banknotes are legal tender to an unlimited extent and coins to some limited amounts.

c Token money is money which functions perfectly well as a medium of exchange, but is not legal tender. Bank deposits are a form of token money.

4 Deposits in building societies do not function as a medium of exchange. In recent years, some building societies have introduced a form of deposit on which cheques may be drawn. Such deposits will act as a medium of exchange.

5 Bank deposits.

6 The bank's liabilities increase because the borrower receives a bank deposit which is a claim on the bank. Its assets increase because the loan is a claim on the borrower.

7 **a** The banks maintain an extremely small cash ratio because most depositors make payments by cheque and, on any given day, withdrawals of cash are likely to be balanced by deposits of cash.

b No. The banks' liabilities (deposits) are balanced by assets of equal value, but most of these assets earn income and are not perfectly liquid.

8 **a** The individual bank will re-lend 90 per cent of the new deposit and hence create additional bank deposits of £9000.

b The banking system as a whole will be able to use the £10 000 cash to support £100 000 of bank deposits. Hence the money supply will increase by £90 000 (in the form of additional bank deposits).

9 Banks compete to attract funds because these can be on-lent at higher rates of interest than those paid to depositors. The inter-bank market helps to remove surpluses and shortages within the banking system: banks with surpluses lend to banks with shortages.

10 A large percentage of cheques made out on any one day will be drawn on accounts in one bank but payable to accounts in a different bank. This means that deposits must move from one bank to another. The *clearing arrangements* enable banks to offset their claims against each other so that relatively small payments are needed to settle the *net* difference. Clearing banks make payments to one another by using their accounts at the Bank of England, so that if one bank is persistently indebted to other banks it will find its cash reserves falling.

11 **a** Notes and coin and operational balances at the Bank of England.
b Cash is an asset which earns no income.

c

Liabilities	£ million	Assets	£ million
Deposits	20 000	Cash	2 000
		Securities	6 750
		Loans	11 250
	20 000		20 000

12 Banks are joint stock companies and have an obligation to earn profits for their shareholders. They also have an obligation to depositors to meet all demands for cash. The first obligation leads them to acquire more profitable assets in the form of longer-term (but illiquid) loans. The second obligation requires them to hold adequate supplies of liquid assets in the form of short-term (but less profitable) loans.

13 Treasury bills, local authority bills, commercial bills, certificates of deposit and government securities with less than one year to run to maturity.

14 Treasury bills are issued weekly and sold by tender (a form of auction). All the bills on offer are sure to be taken up because the discount houses agree to *underwrite* the tender.

15 Eligible bills are those bills which are eligible for rediscount at or sale to the Bank of England. They consist of Treasury bills, local authority bills and commercial bills accepted by eligible banks (i.e. banks whose status is acceptable to the Bank of England).

16 **a** Rate of discount $= \frac{£200}{£5000} \times \frac{100}{1} \times \frac{4}{1}$

$= 16.0\%$

b Rate of interest $= \frac{£200}{£4800} \times \frac{100}{1} \times \frac{4}{1}$

$= 16.66\%$

17 **a** Cash ratio deposits are the non-interest bearing balances which must be held at the Bank of England by all institutions in the monetary sector (except the Bank of England itself) which have eligible liabilities of £10 million or more. In 1983, cash ratio deposits were fixed at 0.5 per cent of a bank's eligible liabilities.

b Operational deposits are the working balances held by banks (mainly clearing banks) at the Bank of England.

c Special deposits are a major instrument of monetary policy. When requested to do so, the banks must place specified amounts of money into a special account at the Bank of England. These deposits earn interest but are not part of the banks' liquidity.

18 a (i) M1 (ii) £M3

b Although the basic function of money is to act as a medium of exchange, it is difficult to decide how money should be defined for purposes of monetary policy. 'Spending power' can be held in a whole range of financial assets which act as stores of wealth but can easily and quickly be converted into notes, coin and sight deposits. These assets possess varying degrees of liquidity and there is a problem in deciding where to draw the line when defining those assets that are most closely related to changes in expenditure. It is necessary to have several monetary aggregates because any one measure may be affected by special factors. For example, an increase in the rate of interest may slow down the growth of sight deposits, but this might be misleading because money balances are probably being transferred to time deposits (which are included in £M3). Another factor in choosing between different monetary aggregates for purposes of monetary policy is the central bank's ability to control the items to be included in the aggregate.

c Time deposits earn interest whereas, generally speaking, sight deposits do not.

Multiple choice questions

19 E **20** C **21** D **22** B **23** C **24** C **25** C **26** A **27** C

True or false?

28 a False **b** True **c** True **d** False **e** True **f** False **g** False
h True **i** False **j** False

Data response questions

29 a At times when government revenue is greatly exceeding government expenditure, a large surplus is not allowed to develop in the government's account. Any surplus funds are used to reduce government borrowings, in an attempt to keep down the cost of interest charges on public debt.

b (i) In the Issue Department return,
'Notes in Banking Department' rises to £14 million and
'Government securites' rises to £3227 million.

In the Banking Department return,
'Notes and coin' rises to £14 million and
'Government securities' falls to £446 million (they are transferred to the Issue Department in exchange for the notes).

(ii) In the Banking Department return,
'Bankers' deposits' falls to £547 million and
'Public deposits' rises to £141 million.

(iii) In the Issue Department return,
'Notes in circulation' rises to £11 273 million and
'Notes in Banking Department' falls to £2 million.
In the Banking Department return,
'Bankers' deposits' falls to £645 million and
'Notes and coin' falls to £2 million.

(iv) In the Banking Department return,
'Special deposits' rises to £100 million and
'Bankers' deposits' falls to £547 million.

30 a 'The maturing of earlier assistance to the market' means that loans made by the Bank of England at an earlier time became due for repayment. The repayment of these loans reduced the bankers' (including the discount houses') balances at the central bank, thus leaving the banking system short of cash.

'The seasonal strength of Exchequer finances' refers to the fact that at certain times of the year tax revenues significantly exceed government outlays. This net flow of funds to the Exchequer will reduce the bankers' balances at the Bank of England, and hence the liquidity of the banks.

b Cash shortages in the money market may be relieved by the Bank of England supplying the necessary cash to the market by means of (i) purchases of eligible bills or (ii) loans against the security of such bills. These actions would increase the current balances held by money market institutions in the central bank.

c The 'base rate' is the lowest rate of interest charged on loans by the banks. It applies only to the most credit-worthy borrowers (e.g. public authorities).

The quotation indicates that rather than taking positive action to manipulate the market rate of interest at this time, the central bank was allowing market forces to determine interest rates.

Answers to part 5

Short answer questions

1 Generally speaking, it can be said that an asset is more liquid the more swiftly it can be *converted into the means of payment*, and the more certain its *monetary value*.

2 'Liquidity preference' refers to people's demand for money to hold, that is, the demand for money as an asset.

3 The symbol *a* represents the average number of times each unit of money is used in the purchase of final goods and services. In other words, *a* stands for the income velocity of circulation of money.

4 If people wish to hold a relatively small amount of money, then most of the money they receive will be spent (i.e. passed on to others), and money will circulate rapidly. If they wish to hold relatively large amounts of money, money will circulate more slowly. Thus, with a given stock of money, the greater the demand for money (i.e. the lower is V), the lower will be the level of expenditure. (V is the velocity of circulation of money.)

5 The *transactions* demand for money arises because people need to have a stock of the medium of exchange to undertake day-to-day purchases of goods and services. The *precautionary* demand for money arises because a certain amount of money needs to be held to deal with unexpected and unforeseen expenditures.

6 If the rate of interest is expected to rise (i.e. security prices are expected to fall), holders of fixed-interest securities face the prospect of capital losses. In such circumstances, holding cash rather than securities means forgoing the interest on securities, but this may mean a much smaller loss than the fall in the capital value of the securities if the rate of interest does increase.

7 The annual income from a fixed-interest bond is fixed in terms of money. Thus, if the *market price* of such a bond falls, the *yield* on that bond (i.e. the market rate of interest) will rise. For example, if the market price of a 10% bond (nominal value £100) falls from £80 to £60, the yield rises from

$$\frac{£10}{£80} \times \frac{100}{1} = 12\tfrac{1}{2}\%$$

to $$\frac{£10}{£60} \times \frac{100}{1} = 16.6\%$$

8 The velocity of circulation of money.

9 It is reasonable to assume that firms and households rarely borrow money unless they intend to spend it. Any change in bank lending, therefore, should have fairly predictable effects on expenditure.

10 In order to restrict the growth of the stock of money, the monetary authorities will probably aim to raise the market rate of interest (to reduce the demand for bank loans). A relatively high rate of interest in the UK, however, will tend to attract funds from abroad and this will have the effect of raising the external value of the pound sterling.

11 The advantage of direct controls is that their effect on bank lending is fairly predictable.

The disadvantages of direct controls are that (i) borrowers may bypass the controls by approaching lenders other than the banks subject to the controls, and (ii) such controls inhibit competition between the banks.

12 Other things being equal, in order to persuade people to hold a larger stock of government securities, higher interest rates on these securities will be required.

13 The controls were most effective in restricting the demand for consumer durables, although hire-purchase is important in the market for capital goods. Demand is restricted by increasing the amount of the initial deposit and by shortening the period allowed for the repayment of the loan. Reversing these measures leads to an expansion of demand.

14 The central bank can influence the market rate of interest by open market operations. For example, substantial sales of securities will lower their market prices and hence raise the market rate of interest. Open market purchases will tend to have the opposite effect. The Bank of England can also influence market rates of interest by varying the terms on which it is prepared to offer financial assistance to the money market.

15 The size of the PSBR is determined by government policies on public spending and taxation (i.e. fiscal policy). The way the PSBR is financed can affect the money supply in different ways, depending on the extent to which the funds are obtained by borrowing from the banking system or from the non-bank public. Sales of securities to the non-bank public will tend to restrict the growth of the money supply (see the answer to question **16b**); borrowing from the banks will tend to increase the money supply.

16 **a** See the answer to question **14**.

b Payments for the securities will involve a transfer of funds from the commercial banks to the Bank of England. This reduces the liquidity of the banks and hence limits their ability to lend (i.e. to create bank deposits).

17 The completed table is shown below.

Instruments	**Operating target**	**Intermediate target**	**Objective**
Open market operations Special deposits Central bank's lending rate	Liquidity of the banking system	The growth of the money supply	Reducing the rate of inflation by controlling aggregate money demand

Multiple choice questions

18 A **19** D **20** B **21** C **22** A **23** D **24** C **25** D **26** D

True or false?

27 a True **b** False **c** False **d** True **e** True **f** False **g** False
h True

Data response questions

28 a

Central Bank

Liabilities		Assets	
Bankers' deposits	+100m.	Securities	+100m.

Commercial Banks

Liabilities		Assets	
Deposits	+£100m.	Balances at central bank	+£100m.

Households

Liabilities		Assets	
		Securities	−£100m.
		Bank deposits	+£100m.

b Other things being equal, bank deposits will expand by some multiple of £100 million. The extent of the expansion depends upon the liquidity ratio adopted by the banks and the availability of credit-worthy borrowers.

c

Central Bank

Liabilities		Assets	
Bankers' deposits	−£100m.	Securities	−£100m.

Commercial Banks

Liabilities		Assets	
Deposits	−£100m.	Balances at central bank	−£100m.

Households

Liabilities		Assets	
		Securities	+£100m.
		Bank deposits	+£100m.

d Other things being equal, bank deposits will contract *if* at the time of the sale of securities, the banks were operating with the minimum liquidity ratio. The contraction of bank deposits will be some multiple of £100 million, depending on the liquidity ratio adopted by the banks. The central bank's sale of securities may have little or no effect on bank deposits if the banks have a surplus of liquid assets.

29 Prospective buyers of government securities may be looking for capital gains, or at least be anxious to avoid capital losses. This means that they need to be convinced that there is a strong likelihood that the next movement in security prices will be upwards (i.e. that interest rates will fall rather than rise). Hence, relatively high interest rates may be deliberately engineered in order to persuade prospective buyers that security prices are about to rise.

30 **a** Reducing the rate of inflation calls for deflationary monetary measures, that is, restraints on bank lending and relatively high interest rates. Investment (and hence, growth) will be discouraged by the lack of availability of funds and the high cost of borrowing.

b See the answer to question **15**. Also see question **28c** (and its answer).

c Investment and growth may be encouraged by relatively low interest rates and by measures which encourage the banks to increase their lending. Low interest rates, however, may persuade foreign holders of funds in London to withdraw these funds and move them to other financial centres where interest rates are higher. Such a trend will tend to depress the external value of the pound. Measures to encourage growth by expanding aggregate demand may generate inflationary pressures which cause balance of payments difficulties. This also may persuade overseas holders of funds in London to withdraw them because they will anticipate a depreciation of the pound sterling.

31 **a** (i) When the central bank purchases eligible bills from institutions in the monetary sector (e.g. the discount houses) the composition of the assets held by these institutions changes: holdings of bills decline and deposits at the central bank increase.

(ii) Since customers' deposits are unaffected by these transactions, the liabilities' side of the balance sheet is unaffected.

b (i) An increase in the rate of interest increases the opportunity cost of holding money balances and will tend to reduce the demand for money to hold. A fall in the rate of interest will have the opposite effect. Expectations regarding changes in the rate of interest will influence the speculative demand for money. If interest rates are expected to rise (i.e. security prices are expected to fall), there will be an increase in the demand for money. The opposite will apply if interest rates are expected to fall.

(ii) The rate of interest is the price of loans. An increase in the cost of borrowed funds will reduce the demand for loans since some projects which were marginally profitable at the lower rate will not be proceeded with at the higher rate. A fall in the rate of interest will increase the demand for loans since some projects which were unattractive at the higher rate of interest will now appear more promising.

(iii) The exchange rate is affected by the rate of interest because there is a large volume of money which is very mobile internationally. Funds will tend to move from one financial centre to another, seeking (among other things) a higher rate of return. Thus, relatively high interest rates in London will attract funds from abroad while relatively low rates will cause such funds to be withdrawn. These movements affect the supply of and demand for pounds in the foreign exchange market, and hence the rate of exchange.

Answers to part 6

Short answer questions

1 $MV = PQ$

If V remained constant, then MV must have increased by 10 per cent. If expenditure (MV) increased by 10 per cent and output (Q) increased by 12 per cent, prices must have changed in the ratio 112:110, i.e. in the ratio 100:98.2. Prices fell by approximately 1.8 per cent.

2 The *transactions* velocity refers to the rate at which money changes hands when all transactions are taken into account (i.e. transactions in final goods and services *and* intermediate goods and services). The *income* velocity refers to the rate at which money changes hands in those transactions which are included in the national income calculations (i.e. transactions in final goods and services).

3 Prices represent incomes, so that if there is a rise in the *general price level*, there is also a rise in money incomes and hence an increase in aggregate money demand. In effect, rising prices generate the ability to pay the higher prices.

4 (i) An increase in exports not offset by an increase in imports (or some other leakage).

(ii) An increase in investment not offset by an increase in saving or taxation.

(iii) An increase in government spending on goods and services not offset by a fall in private spending.

(iv) An increase in the average propensity to consume.

(v) According to the monetarists, the main cause is the money supply being allowed to rise faster than the country's productive potential.

5 **a** (Keynesian theory) The increase in M would cause people to buy bonds in attempts to shed their excess liquidity (bonds are regarded as very close substitutes for money). Bond prices would rise and the rate of interest would fall. Since the demand for money is believed to be interest rate elastic, a relatively small fall in the rate of interest would be sufficient to persuade people to hold a larger quantity of money. Spending on consumer durables and capital goods is regarded by Keynesians as being interest rate inelastic, so that a relatively large fall in the rate of interest would be required to bring about any significant change in this type of expenditure.

b (Monetarist theory) The increase in M would have a relatively large effect on the rate of interest because money is demanded mainly for transactions purposes. An increase in M will not bring about an immediate and relatively large increase in the demand for bonds because bonds are not regarded as such close substitutes for money as the Keynesians maintain.

Thus it will require a relatively large fall in the rate of interest to persuade people to hold more money; the demand for money is interest rate inelastic.

The fall in the rate of interest will lead to a substantial increase in the demand for consumer durables and capital goods since the demand for these items is very sensitive to changes in interest rates, although there may be a fairly long time-lag.

6 The 10% increase in prices will lead to a 10% rise in wages and hence costs (and prices) will rise by 7%. This 7% rise in prices will cause wages to rise by 7% and this, in turn, will raise costs (and prices) by 4.9%. This is a diminishing series.

7 It is likely to be a major factor in causing average wage rates to rise faster than average increases in productivity. If workers in a major industry achieve a wage increase greater than the average increase in productivity, either because productivity in their own industry has risen by more than the national average or because they are in a very strong bargaining position, then workers in other industries are likely to demand similar wage increases in order to maintain existing differentials.

8 Rising prices will increase the demand for money (for transactions purposes). If interest rates are not to move upwards, the central bank will be obliged to increase the supply of money.

9 **a** (i) The slope of the line *OR* (i.e. *RA*/*OA*).

(ii) The slope of the line *OS* (i.e. *SB*/*OB*).

(iii) As output increases up to *OA*, it is assumed that output can be increased to meet the increased demand (i.e. there are unemployed resources in this output range) and prices will not increase.

(iv) *OC* represents the full-employment output.

b An increase in productive potential due to factors such as (i) increases in the stock of capital, (ii) increases in the supply of and/or the efficiency of labour and (iii) technical progress.

10 **a** An increase in the average propensity to consume, an increase in the rate of investment, an increase in government spending on goods and services (rates of taxation remaining unchanged) or an increase in exports.

b It would remain unchanged because the *Z* curve is a straight line over the corresponding increase in output.

c (i) Planned money expenditures exceed the total expenditure required to persuade firms to produce the output *OB*.

(ii) Income and output will expand because profits will increase and this will encourage firms to increase production.

d It will increase from the slope of the line *OG* to the slope of the line *OF*.

11 (i) The marginal propensity to consume tends to fall as income increases.

(ii) Direct taxation will tend to be progressive.

(iii) Rising prices may reduce the demand for exports and increase the demand for imports.

(iv) A fall in *X* (exports) and an increase in *M* (imports) will reduce the rate of growth of aggregate demand.

(v) Rising prices will tend to increase the rate of interest which will tend to reduce the rate of investment.

12 Price expectations become increasingly important as people learn to live with inflation. They will become an important component in trade union wage claims and firms' willingness to grant wage increases will probably be influenced by their expectations of price increases in the future.

13 If prices and wages increase steadily, the demand for money will also increase. If the supply of money is kept unchanged there will be an upward movement in interest rates which will reduce output and employment. This fall in output will reduce aggregate demand and bring the inflationary process to a halt. By increasing the money supply, the government 'sanctions' the wage and price increases.

14 The answer is based on the graph below.

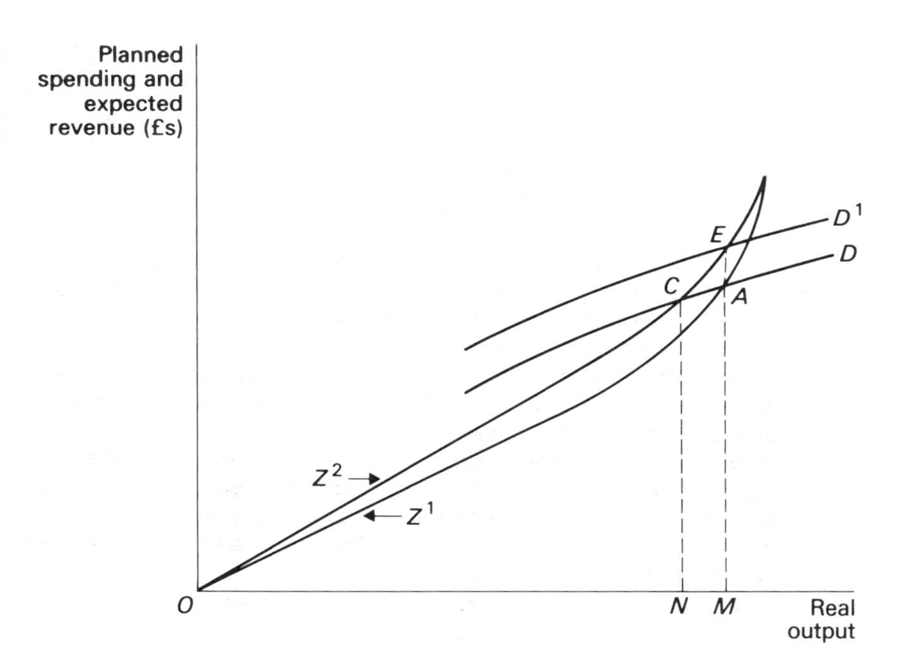

The increase in the costs of production has moved the aggregate supply curve from Z^1 to Z^2. The effect of this change has been to increase the general price level from slope *OA* to slope *OC*. If demand does not change, output will fall to *ON*, but this does not happen because the increase in costs represents an increase in incomes so that aggregate money demand will increase. If demand increases to D^1, there will be a new equilibrium at output *OM* but at a higher price level (slope *OE*). But this position is not stable because the further rise in prices will stimulate a further round of wage increases and the process will be repeated.

15 **a** The velocity of circulation of money is stable.
b When the stock of money increases to *OY*, it is greater than the amount which people are willing to hold at the existing level of GNP (i.e. $BA = OX$). People will, therefore, spend their 'surplus' money balances on goods and services. The increase in aggregate demand will increase nominal GNP until it reaches a level where the demand for money is equal to the supply of money (*OY*). The increase in GNP will be mainly in real terms if there are unemployed resources; it will take the form of price increases if there is no excess capacity.

16 The velocity of circulation of money is stable or at least behaves in a predictable manner.

Multiple choice questions

17 C **18** D **19** A **20** E **21** E **22** D **23** C **24** D

True or false?

25 **a** False **b** True **c** False **d** False **e** False **f** False **g** False **h** True **i** True

Data response questions

26 The increase in aggregate demand will increase output, and unemployment will fall. The increase in demand, however, will cause some upward movement in prices. The economy will move up the P_2 curve until it reaches the point where unemployment is at the 3 per cent level, but the rate of inflation is now 4 per cent per annum. For a time employers will have been prepared to increase output in response to the increased demand because wages will not have adjusted to the change in the rate of inflation (the existing rate was set in expectation of a 2 per cent rate of inflation). In relation to the prices of the products, therefore, real wages will have fallen and production becomes more profitable. But workers will eventually respond to the increased rate of inflation by demanding higher money wages in order to restore the former level of real wages. Costs of production will then increase and production becomes less profitable. Firms will react to the fall in profitability by reducing output. The economy will move back to the output determined by the natural rate of unemployment, but at the higher level of inflation (4 per cent). Both firms and workers have now adjusted to the change in the rate of inflation and the existing rate (4 per cent) now becomes the expected rate. If there are no further attempts to increase aggregate demand, the economy settles into equilibrium at the natural rate of unemployment with a stable rate of inflation of 4 per cent.

27 (i) It seems that claims for wage increases have become much more responsive to price changes as people have learned to live with inflation. Wage claims take far more account of expected changes in prices than they did when inflation was moderate.
(ii) After the mid-1960s and particularly in the 1970s there was a significant increase in trade union militancy in the wage bargaining process. Rising unemployment, for a time at least, appeared to have little effect on union pressures for higher wages.
(iii) The relationship portrayed by the Phillips curve appears to be more appropriate to inflation which is caused by excess demand. When inflation is caused by cost-push pressures, the relationship does not appear to hold, or if it does, the increases in cost, not related directly to the level of demand, have moved the Phillips curve a long way to the right.

28 In the light of the figures presented in the table it is difficult to attribute the inflation experienced in the 1970s to excess demand. There was a strong upward trend in the rate of unemployment and vacancies generally were at a very low level.

One factor which does stand out clearly is the very significant increase in import prices, most particularly during the mid-1970s. There is clearly a relationship between the large increases in import prices and the relatively large increase in wage rates which, to some extent, were a response to the rising prices caused by higher import costs.

The increases in import prices were due mainly to shifts in *world* commodity prices but UK import prices also rose because of the fall in the external value of the pound sterling. The depreciation of sterling was itself partly a consequence of the relatively high rates of inflation being experienced in the UK.

There also seems little doubt that wage-push factors were an important contributory factor to the inflationary process and this is supported by the relatively large number of days lost due to industrial disputes (much higher on average than the number of days lost in the 1960s). Many of these disputes may have been due to the rising rate of inflation itself and to attempts to recover 'ground lost' during the periods when incomes policies were in operation.

The increased rates of inflation in the 1970s were accompanied by marked increases in the supply of money. Some economists have interpreted the relationship as one of cause and effect: the increase in the money supply *caused* the increase in the rate of inflation. Others, while admitting that an increase in the money supply can lead to higher prices, point out that it does so by increasing aggregate demand. The data in the table do not provide evidence of excess demand, but many economists are prepared to admit that if the money supply had not been allowed to increase so fast, inflation would have been less severe.

Answers to part 7

Short answer questions

1 If $Y > (C + I + G)$, national output is greater than home demand and the balance of payments will be in surplus. Alternatively,

since $Y = C + I + G + X - M$

then $Y - (C + I + G) = X - M$

If $Y > (C + I + G)$, then $X > M$.

2 In order to make the balance of payments account sum exactly to zero, the withdrawal of funds from the official reserves (in order to cover a deficit) must appear with a positive sign.

3 The items in the official financing section of the balance of payments are transactions which the authorities *are obliged to make* in order to bring about an accounting balance. These transactions are largely the *result* of discrepancies between the inflows and outflows of foreign currency resulting from autonomous transactions.

4 It balances the discrepancy between (i) the totals of *recorded* expenditures on and income from international transactions, and (ii) the changes in financial balances which have been brought about by *all the transactions* which have taken place. Some transactions will not have been recorded and some errors will have been made in the records of imports and exports.

5 **a** Invisibles.
b Invisibles.
c Official financing.
d Capital account.

6 **a** +£1650 million
b +£1150 million
c (i) −£300 million (ii) +£1100 million
d The balance for official financing.

7 The term *non-market balance* refers to a situation where the balance of payments is in equilibrium (i.e. the outflow and inflow on the current plus capital accounts are equal) but where this balance has been obtained by the imposition of restrictions on the operation of market forces. The use of exchange controls, tariffs and quotas, the subsidisation of exports and severe restrictions of home demand would be examples of measures used to achieve a non-market balance.

8 As the oil began to flow from the North Sea, the returns on the foreign capital invested in the development of the oilfields began to build up. The income on this investment in the form of interest, profits and dividends which is being withdrawn from the UK by foreign firms appears as a debit item in the invisibles account.

9 *Depreciation* describes the fall in the external value of a currency when that currency is floating. *Devaluation* is an administered change in the external value of a currency from one fixed rate of exchange to a new and lower rate.

10 In terms of dollars, the value of goods priced in sterling will change in the ratio 100:90. This means that in terms of pounds, the value of goods priced in dollars changes in the ratio 90:100, i.e. they increase by 11 per cent.

11 The immediate effect of devaluation or depreciation is to reduce the prices of exports in terms of foreign currency. The prices of imports in terms of foreign currency do not change (they rise in terms of the home currency). It will take some time for the volumes of exports and imports to change in response to these price changes. In the short term, therefore, export earnings in foreign currency will fall, while expenditures on imports in foreign currency will remain unchanged. The balance of payments is adversely affected. In the longer term, the volumes of exports and imports will change, and providing the elasticities of demand and supply are favourable, the balance of payments will improve. Plotted on a graph, this deterioration in the external balance followed by a substantial improvement would resemble the letter *J*.

12 **a** $1.0 = 2.5 fr.

b Arbitrage.

c If the speculator changed the francs into dollars, he or she would receive $2000. These dollars could then be exchanged for £1000, which, in turn, could be exchanged for 5000 fr.

13 The unfavourable income effect might arise if devaluation led to a substantial fall in imports. This would reduce other countries' exports and the national incomes of these countries would fall. This would reduce their ability to import.

14 **a** A *reserve currency* is one which is widely used as an international liquid asset. Many countries will hold such a currency as an important component of their official reserves.

b In the normal course of events the supply of dollars as a reserve currency can be increased only by the USA running balance of payments deficits.

15 **a** Special Drawing Rights are an international liquid asset created by the IMF. They are allocated to member countries in proportion to members' quotas.

b The importance of SDRs lies in the fact that the supply can be increased by international agreement in order to keep pace with the growth of world trade. The supply of SDRs is not arbitrary as is the case with a reserve currency (the supply of which depends upon the balance of payments position of the country whose currency is functioning as a reserve currency).

16 An importer faces the risk that, between the time when he places an order and the time when he has to make payment for the goods, the home currency may have depreciated. This will raise his costs in terms of the home currency. This particular risk may be reduced by making use of the *forward market*, where foreign currency may be purchased for future delivery at some guaranteed price.

17 If a country on a fixed exchange rate is suffering from a persistent balance of payments deficit, it must take steps to eliminate the deficit before its attempts to defend the fixed parity exhaust its foreign currency reserves and its borrowing facilities. Measures to deal with the deficit may include
(i) a reduction in aggregate demand (to reduce imports), but this will tend to increase unemployment,
(ii) raising interest rates to encourage an inward flow of foreign capital (or to eliminate an outward flow), but this measure will discourage investment and raise the cost of mortgages,
(iii) the use of import controls which will tend to raise prices at home and may provoke retaliation and
(iv) devaluation, which will raise import prices and may, under conditions of full employment, require the use of unpopular measures to reduce home demand in order to release more goods for export markets.

18 Under a system of fixed exchange rates, a reserve fund of foreign currencies, gold and SDRs is needed for purposes of intervention in the foreign exchange market in order to maintain the fixed parity. If the exchange rate tends to fall, these reserves will be needed in order to purchase the currency (an increase in demand will prevent the price of the currency falling).

When exchange rates are *freely* floating, the market mechanism will function to eliminate surpluses and deficits by changes in price (i.e. the rate of exchange). If countries are practising 'dirty floating', reserves are needed for intervention purposes.

19 (i) When interest rates in the country concerned are significantly higher than in other major financial centres.
(ii) When trade prospects point to a strong balance of payments position in the immediate future and to a possible appreciation of the domestic currency (or to a revaluation).
(iii) When political and economic uncertainty in one or more other countries causes fears of possible depreciation (or devaluation) of other currencies.

20 The basic idea of the Purchasing Power Parity Theory is that in perfectly free markets, the external values of currencies will settle at levels which make the purchasing power of a unit of currency the same wherever it is spent. This means that if £1 = $2.0, then £1 in the UK will buy exactly the same quantity and variety of goods as would $2.0 in the USA.

Multiple choice questions

21 E **22** E **23** E **24** A **25** B **26** B **27** C **28** B **29** A **30** C

True or false?

31 **a** True **b** True **c** True **d** True **e** False **f** False **g** True
h True **i** False **j** True **k** False **l** True

Data response questions

32 **a** When the pound depreciates, UK goods become cheaper in terms of foreign currencies.

b This is best explained by an example. Suppose the pound depreciates from £1 = $1.75 to £1 = $1.50. If UK exporters do not change the sterling prices of their exports, then an article priced at £1000 will fall in price on the USA market from $1750 to $1500.

But if the UK exporter increases his profit margin by raising the sterling price to £1166.60, the dollar price will remain at $1750. Profits will increase, but in this particular case there will be no increase in quantity sold.

c The relevant information is 'British imports rise by 1.6% for every 1% rise in GDP'. This poses a real dilemma for UK governments, because attempts to reduce unemployment by increasing aggregate demand will clearly lead to a substantial increase in imports and to possible serious consequences for the balance of payments.

d A cheaper pound means that the sterling prices of imports will be higher. These higher prices of foodstuffs, raw materials and capital equipment will raise domestic costs and hence increase domestic prices. The relevance of the value of the dollar is that many goods traded in world markets are invoiced in dollars and North America is a relatively important market for UK firms. Thus, if the depreciation of the pound is accompanied by a depreciation of the dollar (against other currencies), the fall in the value of the pound relative to other currencies will not have such serious consequences.

e Other things being equal, a depreciation of the pound will raise the sterling prices of imports. This effect would be modified if importers reduced their profit margins. For example, if the pound fell from £1 = $1.75 to £1 = $1.50, then an American machine priced at $3500 will rise in price on the UK market from £2000 to £2333.30. But if UK importers decided to reduce their profit margins, the rise in the sterling price would be more moderate and the inflationary effects less severe.

33 **a** It is first necessary to divide the quantity of dollars supplied by the appropriate exchange rate in order to obtain the demand schedule for pounds. This demand schedule and the supply schedule for pounds can then be plotted to form the demand and supply curves for pounds as shown in the graph on page 130.

b The equilibrium rate of exchange is £1 = $1.8.

c The monetary authorities must buy £1000 million in order to raise the

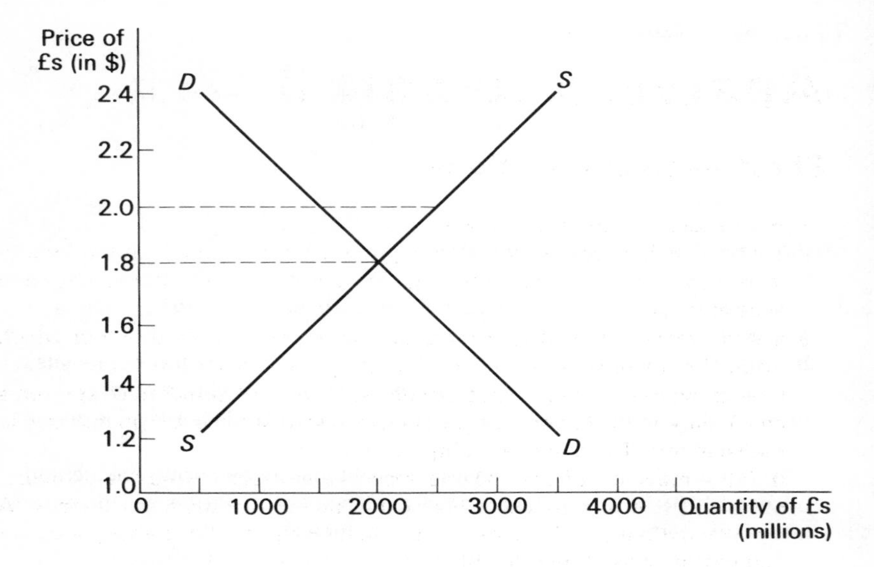

demand for pounds. In buying pounds, the authorities will be spending dollars.

d The Exchange Equalisation Account.

Answers to part 8

Short answer questions

1 **c** Changes in output per capita.

2 This occurs because the gains from growth are taken partly in the form of increased leisure; people tend to spend a shorter portion of their days and lives at work.

3 **a** A movement from *A* to *B* represents an increase in total output which results from a greater utilisation of existing resources; output increases as unemployed resources are put to work. A movement from *B* to *C* represents an increase in the economy's productive potential since it is an increase in the level of full-employment output.

b (ii) A movement from *C* to *E* represents an increase in the rate of investment and this in turn will increase the nation's productive capacity. A movement from *C* to *D* increases the current output of consumer goods but reduces the rate of investment.

4 If a constant level of income is redistributed, some people will suffer a loss of income. If there is economic growth, however, a proportionately greater share of the increase in income can be allocated (by government intervention) to the lower income groups.

5 The rate of capital accumulation can only be increased if there is an increase in the rate of saving. The rate of saving can only be increased (in poor countries) if there is an increase in income, but an increase in income requires an increase in investment!

6 The reallocation of resources from consumer goods industries to capital goods industries results in a fall in the level of consumption. After ten years, the output of consumer goods is restored to the level it would have attained had the reallocation of resources not taken place. The shaded area between the lines over the first ten years represents the loss of consumption over this period. It will, however, be approximately another ten years before consumption over the whole period is as large as it would have been had the rate of growth not been increased.

7 **a** $\frac{Y}{Y_f} \times 100$ represents the percentage utilisation of productive capacity.

b A significant increase in the percentage utilisation of capacity is possible when a relatively large proportion of the economic resources is unemployed.

8 The capital/output ratio is the amount of capital divided by the amount of output. Thus, if £10 000 worth of capital is required to produce an annual output of £5000 worth of goods, the capital/output ratio is 2. If the marginal efficiency (i.e. productivity) of capital is declining (due to diminishing returns) the capital/output ratio will be increasing. For example, it will mean, perhaps, that £12 000 of capital is required to produce £5000 of output.

9 This can be achieved if an increase in the average size of the units of production yields economies of scale.

10 It is the amount by which investment must increase in order to generate the additional income needed to buy the additional output resulting from the net investment of the previous time period.

11 Technical progress offsets the effects of the law of diminishing returns. By increasing the marginal productivity of capital, technical progress causes the MEC curve to move upwards.

Multiple choice questions

12 B **13** C **14** A **15** A

True or false?

16 **a** True **b** True **c** False **d** False **e** True **f** False

Data response question

17 **a** The diagram plots for each country, the amount of investment as a percentage of GDP (for the years 1963–76) against the growth of productivity in manufacturing (for the years 1971–9). The time-lag has some relevance because productivity gains from investment will probably accrue after a time interval of one or two years. The rate of investment in the UK over the time period 1963–76 compared favourably with the rates for Italy, West Germany, France and the USA but much less favourably with the rate achieved by Japan. The gains in productivity, however, were substantially inferior to those achieved by the other countries.

b The causes of the discrepancy highlighted by the diagram are the subject of much dispute. Several factors have been suggested as major causes:

(i) A disproportionate amount of investment has been devoted to industries with little or no growth potential; for example, investment intended to halt or slow down the decline of older, heavily localised, industries.

(ii) Immobilities in the labour force and a reluctance to accept changes in working practices has meant that full advantage has not been taken of new equipment. Fears of redundancy arising from more efficient production methods has sometimes led to overmanning when new machines have been introduced.

(iii) Deficiencies in management and organisation has been a cause of the

under-utilisation of capital. For example, defects in quality control lead to excessive use of resources in remedying faults, and inefficient maintenance organisation means that assembly lines are out of action for a disproportionate amount of the time available for production.
(iv) In some industries the UK has not invested in optimum-sized plants and hence has not obtained the economies of scale achieved by some major competitors.
(v) Over this period, productivity appears to have risen fastest in manufacturing and the UK rate of investment in the industrial sector appears to have been less than in some other countries.

Answers to part 9

Short answer questions

1 Monetarists argue that an expansionary fiscal policy will have relatively little effect on aggregate demand because increased public spending will be largely offset by a decrease in private spending (the 'crowding out' effect). The increase in government spending will be financed by increased borrowing which will tend to raise the rate of interest (via the increased demand for loans). Private spending on capital goods and consumer goods, according to the monetarists, is very sensitive to changes in the rate of interest so that the fall in private spending will be relatively large.

2 Flat-rate increases in income narrow the percentage differentials in incomes. If this process were allowed to continue there would be strong resistance from the higher income groups. The erosion of differentials, it is argued, would weaken the incentive to acquire skills and undertake long periods of training. In other words, it would reduce the supply of skilled labour.

3 This statement is based on the view that the bargaining power of the trade unions is directly related to the level of employment (i.e. the demand for labour). When unemployment is low, unions will be very strong and effectively resist attempts to restrict their bargaining powers. Also, when unemployment is very low, excess demand will cause wage rates to be pulled upwards. When unemployment is high, the argument goes, the power of the unions is weak, the pressure for higher wages diminishes and employers will have little difficulty in ensuring that wage rates do not rise faster than productivity.

4 Some degree of flexibility is necessary because economic conditions and techniques of production are always changing. Movements in wage differentials are necessary to encourage the movement of labour from declining industries to expanding industries. Some incentive in the form of relatively larger pay increases may be necessary in order to encourage improvements in productivity. Workers who do not benefit from these exceptions to the general rule (i.e. the norm) will feel aggrieved and it will be difficult to obtain their cooperation in the operation of a voluntary incomes policy.

5 The abolition of exchange controls removed restrictions on the freedom of UK citizens to invest overseas. At this particular time the pound was appreciating because the increased price of oil had strengthened Britain's trade balance and interest rates in the UK were relatively high. The increased flow of investment overseas increased the supply of pounds in the foreign exchange market and helped to moderate the tendency for the pound to appreciate.

6 As a restrictive measure, monetary policy can be made to work. Increasing restrictions on bank lending and rising interest rates must at some point seriously curtail borrowing and spending. As a stimulating force, the effect of monetary policy is much less certain. Low interest rates and the easy availability of credit will not *necessarily* stimulate spending; it all depends upon whether people take an optimistic or pessimistic view about future events. Monetary policy can be used effectively to enforce a restriction on private spending ('pulling on a string') but it cannot *enforce* an increase in private spending ('pushing on a string').

7 This is an example of the balanced budget multiplier, the value of which is 1. National income will fall by $1 \times \Delta G$; that is, by £1000 million. If we assume that the community's MPC is 0.6, then the cut in taxation will set up a series of increments in spending as follows:

+£600m. + £360m. + £216m. + . . .

The cut in government spending has a downward multiplier effect and income will fall as in the following series:

−£1000m. − £600m. − £360m. − £216m. − . . .

The *net effect* of the two series is a fall in income of £1000 million.

8 **a** Fiscal policy.
b Fiscal policy.
c Monetary policy.
d Exchange rate policy.
e Direct controls.
f Institutional changes.

9 Allowances must be made for (i) increases in productivity, (ii) the proportion of aggregate demand devoted to imports, (iii) immobilities in the labour force and (iv) the extent to which increases in demand are met by extended waiting lists and lengthening order books.

10 (i) Inflation. Increases in aggregate demand which had been mainly job-creating in the 1950s and 1960s were increasingly affecting prices as well as output. Fears of escalating inflation restricted the extent to which governments were prepared to increase demand.
(ii) The drift of some types of industrial production (e.g. cars and textiles) to the less developed countries.
(iii) Immobilities and insufficient innovation. The loss of jobs due to migrating industries was not fully matched by the creation of new jobs. Immobilities and low productivity was probably a deterrent to investment in some industrial sectors of the OECD. (See also question **11**.)

11 **a** Tax thresholds are the levels of taxable income at which the rates of taxation change. For example,

Taxable income (£s)	**Rate of tax**
0–3999	0
4000–5999	35%
6000–7999	40%
8000–9999	45%

During periods of inflation, money incomes will be rising much faster than real incomes. If the tax thresholds are not adjusted to take account of inflation, the rise in money incomes will place people in higher tax brackets and they will be paying a greater portion of their *real* incomes in taxation. This effect together with the higher social security benefits has, according to some commentators, diminished the incentive to take up paid employment.

b This may be explained by means of an example. Suppose that each week, 1000 people lose their jobs and 1000 people find new jobs. If the *average* amount of time spent on the unemployment register is two weeks, the aggregate unemployment figure will be 2000. If, however, *the rates* at which jobs are being lost and found remain the same, but each person on for average now spends four weeks out of work, the unemployment figure will rise to 4000.

12 The equilibrium level of national income occurs when, at the existing price level, aggregate money demand is just sufficient to purchase the whole of the national output.

If, at the current level of prices, aggregate money demand is sufficient to buy more than the full employment output of an economy, then the equilibrium level of income is greater than the full employment level of income. In *real terms*, this level of income is not attainable and there will be an inflationary gap at the full employment level of income. This will lead to a rise in prices; *money income* will increase.

Multiple choice questions

13 C **14** D **15** A **16** D **17** B **18** B **19** C **20** D

True or false?

21 **a** True **b** True **c** False **d** False **e** False **f** True **g** True

Data response questions

22 a In equilibrium,

$$\begin{aligned} Y &= C + I + G \\ &= 0.8 \times 0.8Y + £5000\text{m.} + £4000\text{m.} \\ &= 0.64Y + £9000\text{m.} \\ \therefore\ Y &= £25\,000\text{m.} \end{aligned}$$

Alternatively, in equilibrium,

$$\begin{aligned} I + G &= S + T \\ \therefore\ £5000\text{m.} + £4000\text{m.} &= 0.2 \times 0.8Y + 0.2Y \\ \therefore\ £9000\text{m.} &= 0.36Y \\ \therefore\ Y &= £25\,000\text{m.} \end{aligned}$$

b $\text{Multiplier} = \dfrac{1}{\text{MPS} + \text{MRT}}$

$$= \frac{1}{0.16 + 0.2}$$

$$\approx 2.78$$

c In equilibrium,

$$\begin{aligned} Y &= C + I + G \\ &= 0.64Y + £5000\text{m.} + £5800\text{m.} \\ \therefore\ 0.36Y &= £10\,800\text{m.} \\ \therefore\ Y &= £30\,000\text{m.} \end{aligned}$$

d Initially,

$$\text{Consumption} = 0.8 \times 0.8Y = 0.64 \times £25\,000\text{m.} = £16\,000\text{m.}$$

After increase in income,

$$\text{Consumption} = 0.64 \times £30\,000\text{m.} = £19\,200\text{m.}$$

The increase in consumption is £3200 million.

e Government spending = £5800m.

$$\text{Taxation} = 0.2 \times £30\,000\text{m.} = £6000\text{m.}$$

There is a Budget surplus of £200 million.

23 a The very large rises in oil prices raised costs of production and accelerated cost-push inflation. Many of the oil exporting countries have relatively low propensities to import, with the result that they accumulated very large balance of payments surpluses. It was this withdrawal of income from the oil importing nations which was deflationary. The effect was the same as if the oil importing countries had raised indirect taxes and, instead of returning the tax revenue to the economy in the form of increased government spending, had transferred the tax revenues to the oil exporting countries. Since the demand for oil is relatively inelastic, countries found it difficult to effect any short-term significant cut in oil imports and the increase in oil prices meant that it required a greater volume of exports to pay for any given quantity of oil imports. The effect of this, of course, was a reduction in real income for the oil importers.

b In the aftermath of the first large increase in oil prices, the cost-push inflation which they generated was partially accommodated by governments who tried to maintain the demand for output by allowing money incomes to rise. The claims for higher incomes which followed the rise in prices (caused mainly by the higher cost of oil) were accommodated by allowing the money supply to increase so as to 'finance' the higher incomes.

In the aftermath of the second oil shock, governments pursued a much more restrictive monetary policy; the cost and price increases were not accommodated to the same extent. The effect of exercising tighter control on the growth of the money supply was that price increases led to reductions in the quantities demanded and hence to falls in output and employment.

c The diagram indicates that real earnings in manufacturing increased in 1981–2.